The Engendering God

The Engendering God

Male and Female Faces of God

Carl A. Raschke
Susan Doughty Raschke

Westminster John Knox Press
Louisville, Kentucky

*"I am the Alpha and the Omega," says the Lord God, who
is and who was and who is to come.*

—Rev. 1:8

Scripture quotations are from *The New English Bible,* copyright © The Delegates of Oxford
University Press and The Syndics of the Cambridge University Press, 1961, 1970. Reprinted
by permission.

Book design by Drew Stevens
Cover design by Kim Wohlenhaus

First edition

Published by Westminster John Knox Press
Louisville, Kentucky

This book is printed on acid-free paper that meets the American National Standards
Institute Z39.48 standard. ∞

PRINTED IN THE UNITED STATES OF AMERICA

95 96 97 98 99 00 01 02 03 04 — 10 9 8 7 6 5 4 3 2 1

Library of Congress Cataloging-in-Publication Data

Raschke, Carl A.
    The engendering God : male and female faces of God / Carl A.
Raschke, Susan Doughty Raschke. — 1st ed.
        p.   cm.
    Includes bibliographical references.
    ISBN 0-664-25502-7 (alk. paper)
    1. Masculinity of God.   2. Femininity of God.   3. Masculinity of God—Biblical
teaching.   4. Femininity of God—Biblical teaching.   5. Masculinity of God—History of
doctrines.   6. Femininity of God—History of doctrines.   I. Raschke, Susan Doughty.
II. Title.
BT153.F3R37   1995
231'.4—dc20
                                                                                    95-24269

Contents

Preface

This little book is about God, men, and women. It is an effort to come to terms with the meaning of that fateful passage in Genesis: "In the image of God [God] created [humankind]; male and female [God] created them" (Gen. 1:27).

The "them" has always been problematic for a patriarchal theology, as well as for so-called paganism. It applies a unity in duality, a twoness in oneness, a holy and infinite presence that becomes manifest in the finitude of maleness and femaleness, and in the relationship between the two. It is a "paradox" that has not yet been comprehended in its fullness, despite all the efforts in the past thirty years to criticize the androcentrism of historical theology and to make the Christian heritage speak to women.

The thesis of this book is simple and essential, though perhaps radical to many. The thesis is that the scriptures, together with certain key elements of the subsequent Christian tradition, can be *reread* forthrightly to support a conviction of the unconditional religious equality of men and women. This equality is not predicated on some ancillary commitment to political justice or a pragmatic concession to social reality. It hinges on a theological inquiry into the depths of the divine truth and fullness as shown in the very language of scriptural revelation that is frequently used, blasphemously and idolatrously, to preserve certain human institutions that deny dignity to half the human race.

It should be made clear at the outset, however, that the theses and issues contained in this work are, and are likely to remain for some time, controversial. They might even be called speculative. There are indeed entrenched companies of scholars—both to the left and to the right of the theological spectrum—who are certain to differ decidedly with what this book propounds.

In our estimation that penchant is an asset rather than a liability. Both the study of religion and the history of biblical interpretation have been wafted for centuries by cultural fashion and shifting social valuations. The current era is no exception. Every generation reads the ensemble of ancient texts and fragmentary historical and material evidence with a perspective that buttresses the received opinion.

At the turn of the century it would have been impossible to trek through the Bible without encountering at every bend and twist of narrative the "moral authority" of Jesus. In the postwar period one always found oneself gaping at the empty tomb and the mystery of divine action amid the interstices of time and human mortality. In the 1960s the scriptures became a kind of "canon" for political activism that latter was known as liberation theology. Since about the 1980s we have witnessed the rise to power of the so-called new historicists who lay on the act of reading a heavy hand of sociological relativism and an adoration for archaeological remains.

The Engendering God takes a tack that is both bold and unprecedented. Let us call it unashamedly a "theological" thought experiment which, while relying carefully on established research and a broad consensus among scholars concerning what happened or did not happen in the past, weaves together the threads of historic faith with contemporary academic insights into the ancient world.

One of the challenges and struggles facing biblical studies in the twentieth century entails exploration of the uncharted territory where the anthropology of religions mingles with the linguistic and historical analysis of biblical tradition and texts. The problem is far more acute than both experts and laypersons realize. Because of Western civilization's devotion to the divine word contained in scripture and its disfavor toward the heathen religions, which Jewish-Christian monotheism in many cases forcefully replaced, the tendency has been to treat ancient religions as if they were for the most part monolithic in character, if not in number. The old clerical notion of paganism, referring to any European or Mediterranean practice or ceremony that predated Christianity, attests to this ambiguity.

Indeed, the lush variety of ancient religions has rendered the means of interpreting them exceedingly difficult. The religious life of antiquity was widely distinguished by a process known as syncretism, in which random religious structures, beliefs, symbols, and patterns of behavior coalesce into new forms of the sacred. Today we would call this form a cult, a word actually derived from a respectable Latin term designating a passing and episodic type of religious devotion. Because representatives of both ancient Judaism and the early church saw themselves as custodians of a unified spiritual legacy reaching back into the distant past, an appreciation of how important syncretic trends were in the formation of ancient piety has been missing from the beginning.

At the same time, it has been recognized by scholars for more than a generation now that the evolution of Jewish-Christian monotheism also bears in certain measure the signature of syncretism. The intense syncretism of medieval Christianity has long been understood by church historians, but these same processes have been ignored in the examination of the scriptural canon. The dominance of biblical scholarship over the past two centuries by Protestant theology with its rigorous adherence to the majesty and sovereignty of God has contributed to this oversight. The classical notion of the Bible as a continuous narrative that unfolds what the Germans call *Heilsgeschichte,* "sacred history"—the story of God's mysterious plan and dealings with his chosen people—has also enforced such a reading.

One must, however, learn to separate theological conviction from attention to culture and language. Many strange and indecipherable references or prophecies in the Bible, especially in the Old Testament, are known to comprise allusions to these pagan antiquities now lost or obscured. It is a commonplace that early Christian thought, primarily under the influence of Paul, combined the narrative terminology and rhetoric of rabbinic Judaism with the symbolism of the Greek mystery religions that originally focused on reverence for dying and rising gods, and on certain goddesses.

Most of us are theologically sophisticated enough these days to recognize that a historical grasp of how the biblical writers were affected by these cultural externalities does not prejudice necessarily, either for or against, the stance of historic faith. Every age requires that revelation be clothed in the semantic garb with which it is familiar, and in which it is often overdressed. Ancient times were no exception.

But, strangely, while we have been diligent in acknowledging the syncretism of the New Testament writers and in the development of early Christian literature, we have been far more reluctant to identify it in the background of Jesus himself. This reluctance may have something to do with the way Christian minds respectfully, or disrespectfully, read Judaism.

For well nigh two millennia Christian preachers and scholars have stereotyped ancient Judaism in order both to villify it and to provide a straw man for the assertion of the uniqueness of Christianity. The conventional Sunday school catechism, "although Jesus was the Messiah prophesied in the scriptures, he was rejected by his own people," has weighed far more heavily in the misreading of both Testaments than most contemporaries would care to admit. This line of argument, which has become almost unconscious folk wisdom, makes the inherently false assumption that ancient Judaism too was monolithic and immune to syncretism, which the history of religions knows certainly *not* to have been the case.

This book poses very troubling questions without answering them decisively: Could the mission of Jesus and the rhetoric of the early church be the direct descendant of a form of heterodox Judaism, or at least a recognized and authoritative rival to the politically dominant parties at the time of the Caesars that collaborated with the Roman government? Could this strand of ancient Hebraic religion, which is becoming increasingly recognizable by contemporary scholarship, but has not yet been precisely named, also be the missing link between what we know from the literary record as prophetic Judaism and Jesus and his followers? Could the discovery of such a missing link constitute a dangerous threat to certain ensconced religious interests because it would (1) reveal the spurious nature of the ancient rupture between Jews and Christians and (2) both blow apart the patriarchal heritage of the church influenced by the values of Greeks, Romans, and Germans and at the same time give the lie to trendy postmodernist notions that Christianity is a faith that enslaves rather than liberates women and does not assert their equality with men?

This book is an effort to think the unthought both about gender and about Christianity. It is not meant to prove a case. It is only intended to redirect our reflection, as well as our passions and energies, in addressing the inescapable and perennial question concerning the faces of God. The question, as we will argue, is more than academic. As we draw near the millennium, the question may even be called eschatological, inasmuch as it touches directly on the end toward which both faith and understanding of the divine workings are drawn.

The Engendering God takes strands and filaments of historical understanding that have been left in the dark—the "stone which the builders rejected"—and compresses them into a new and dramatic whole. We do not anticipate quick or easy agreement. We realize that, although our perspective is by no stretch of the imagination idiosyncratic and we have been careful to scrutinize to the maximum the diversity of scholarly literature and minute trajectories of research, there persist multiple means of explaining what the data signify. And there are, to be sure, conflicts among different scholarly camps concerning what might be called consensus, and what might not.

For example, our claim that blood sacrifice was practiced within the ritual complex belonging to neolithic matriarchy is one that would have been taken as a matter of course a generation ago, but now has been challenged, despite the testimony of ancient writers, by younger, more politically correct scholars with a vested interest in sustaining the fiction of a benign spectrum of pre-Christian pluralism.

On the other hand, the connection of the teachings of Jesus with the Sophia, or wisdom, tradition of the Old Testament is now virtually quite incontrovertible, particularly in the light of the work of such eminent scholars as Elisabeth Schüssler Fiorenza at Harvard. The issue remains to what degree this tradition is actual legacy or merely a literary genre.

And finally, eschatological books such as the Apocalypse of John have wrongly been read by scholars as either weird and insane ravings or as coded political commentary on happenings in the Roman Empire. We argue that they are neither. They represent the veiling of certain themes and symbols for the hidden stream within both Judaism and Christianity that we call Sophian.

It is simple hope that when all is said and done, scales will fall from many eyes, and the "book of life" will be opened. And the living God will be known as the "engendering God" as well!

C.A.R.
S.D.R.

1

The Engendering Godhead

*So God created [humankind] in [God's] own image; in
the image of God [God] created [humankind]; male and
female [God] created them.*—Gen. 1:27, marg.

As one millennium passes over into the next, the crisis of traditional belief in the Christian world looms larger and larger.

That crisis has many roots. Yet the one overarching problem that will not go away—and perhaps can never be resolved by the usual kinds of theological apologetics and doctrinal tinkering that has characterized modern religious thought—is *God's gender.*

Since the late 1960s, waves of cultural fads and enthusiasms have washed over the wreckage of what was once a proud, Protestant position of prominence within American religion. Out of this wreckage, however, has emerged a very important consensus.

It is the consensus that, in the light of the social revolution under way since the nineteenth century to bring women into an equal relationship *and partnership* with men, we must now undertake a thorough reevaluation of the very biblical symbols on which the timeless Christian faith has rested.

The recurrent attacks of religious feminists on the patriarchal constitution of the church, its doctrines, and its views on biblical authority have masked a deeper issue. Attempts to rewrite the liturgies, and to translate anew the scriptures so that the Christian Deity is no longer exclusively male have failed to grapple with a rudimentary dilemma—*the incommensurability between the concepts and symbols comprising the Western theological tradition and the hidden reality and fullness of the divine itself.*

Women increasingly—and rightfully—have felt disenfranchised from traditional Christianity because of what is perceived as the maleness of its oratory and imagery. This maleness was not a matter of concern, so long as the social equality itself of the sexes was not a critical issue. But it has become increasingly evident to both pastors and academic authors that what appears as a specifically androcentric or "male-gendered" religious heritage cannot carry on unquestioned when women are no longer regarded as inferior to men.

Traditions cannot and should not be altered for casual or transitory reasons. But traditions are never inflexible, and there is a point beyond which changes in social expectations cannot be treated independently

1

of religious values. Such a shift happened during the sixteenth century in Europe when the Protestant Reformation coincided with the breakdown of the feudal society of the Middle Ages. New ideals of individual liberty and the sovereignty of personal conscience were mirrored in the general attack on the monopolistic power of the Roman Catholic Church and its claim to have vested the keys to eternal life and the salvation of souls through a priestly bureaucracy.

Unfortunately, much of the current religious debate over the need to enfranchise women spiritually as well as politically and socially has proceeded from misplaced premises. It has been assumed that the Bible—the wellspring of the Christian faith—is prima facie a patriarchal document.

Such an argument rides on the patent observation that the language of the Bible, and the Old Testament in particular, reflects an obsolete social system in which men ruled the roost and women were breeding stock.

The interconnection between the messages of scripture and everyday forms of social existence cannot be denied. But the attempt to remove the canonical foundations of Christianity laid two thousand years ago in order to vindicate the aims of a social revolution that has been only a century in the making may turn out to be rather quixotic.

Efforts at "de-canonizing" the Christian canon itself have hinged upon a basic theological mistake. It is the same mistake that lay at the heart of the religious controversies of the sixteenth century, the mistake the church reformer Martin Luther referred to as the founding of the "word of God" on the "word of humanity." Updating such terminology, we may refer to it as the sociological fallacy.

The Nature of Metaphor

The *sociological fallacy* derives from a wrong identification of the metaphoric content of a religious symbol with the essence of the divine itself.

The classic convention of referring to the Christian God as "He" actually belies the transcendent character of God disclosed to Moses on the mountain. In the story in which Moses asks the actual name of God, the LORD is both evasive and elliptical. "God answered, 'I AM; that is who I am'" (Ex. 3:14).

The precise translation of the Hebrew in this passage has confounded and eluded experts for centuries. Perhaps it will continue to perplex them, for the divine name on which the Western religious heritage has been erected can never be rendered into a finite formulation. God does not, interestingly, say anything like "I am He," or "I am He that I am." The voice of the Most High simply avows, "I AM."

The older forms of biblical theology that were contextualized as part of a movement of religious thought earlier this century known as neo-orthodoxy remained adamant that religious expressions, including those signifying gender, could not be regarded as absolute or unconditional.

Indeed, there are numerous passages in both the Old and New Testaments where God is depicted as having feminine as well as masculine qualities.[1] The controversy over the gender of God, which has spilled so much printer's ink in this generation, may turn out to be more a cultural than a theological concern. Biblical thought has always been suspicious of all proclivities of the religious imagination to make the limited language of human experience into statements about God in the ultimate sense. When human beings act on such proclivities, they are guilty of the great *sin of idolatry,* according to biblical writers.

When contemporary apologists sometimes argue that the use of the third-person masculine pronoun in reference to God, together with such patriarchal titles as "Father in heaven," is largely metaphorical rather than *representational,* they have a solid basis within the tradition itself to make such a claim. There is no absolute reason within the tradition itself to talk about God as "He."

Yet the defense launched by the traditionalist position may be increasingly irrelevant. As linguists and behavioral theorists tell us routinely these days, metaphors are neither passive nor inert. They possess power to shape the perceptions and anticipations of the speaker.

Furthermore, the very principle of metaphoric language implies that there is some kind of correlation between the image evoked by the word or phrase and the reality it encompasses. As far as religious language is concerned, the metaphoric properties of so-called God-talk always bear some integral connection with the sense of who God really is.

This view was established as far back as the thirteenth century by St. Thomas Aquinas, who argued that the terminology we employ to characterize the Deity must be both appropriate and proportionate in its meaning to the true nature of divinity. Thus even if biblical language in essence is conceived as conditioned and metaphoric, the conspicuous absence of what has been identified in the contemporary world as a distinctive quality of human experience—*the experience of women*—cannot be dismissed as a trifle.

The historical reasons for the dearth of feminine language in the Christian tradition are not obvious and are far more complex than many writers today would lead us to think. The popular notion of Christianity as one of the henchmen in a patriarchal conspiracy against women oversimplifies both the history of religions and the history of culture.

Virtually all of recorded human history was patriarchal in tenor up until the twentieth century. Even those historic religions—such as Hinduism or the polytheism of Rome, Greece, and the ancient Near East—where "goddesses" were revered and held sway at times over their masculine consorts, did not correspond with any social system where women enjoyed high status.

In fact, the opposite was often the case. Women in ancient India were for the most part chattel. In patriarchal Judea they were accorded social dignity that relative to the order of the day was quite high.

Many Roman citizens in the days of the empire worshiped striking and awesome goddess figures who had been imported from Asia Minor, different variations on what scholars and archaeologists have named the *Magna Mater,* "Great Mother." But Roman civilization, with the exception of a very narrow circle of the highborn, tended to degrade women.

Indeed, it was because of the comparatively humane treatment of wives exhibited among early Christians in comparison with the Romans that the new faith spread so rapidly in the first three centuries. The majority of the most ardent converts to early Christianity happened to be women. And it was this male-dominated faith that appealed to them because of its unique transcendent and humane qualities, which the goddess religions did not have. In women's eyes the divine had actually given birth to an eternal child in the form of Jesus. Jesus did not just appear on the stage of history. The divine itself had participated in the birth process.

Even in the pagan milieu with its sanctification of female sexuality, women had little to value religiously and hope for. Women gave birth in travail, and like men, were born in travail. Women's everyday life seemed a form of damnation.

The ancient mother-goddess cults were merely consecrations of the blood and violence of earthly sexuality, as normally practiced. Through Christianity women were given the expectation of receiving spiritual bodies and released from becoming prisoners of their own anatomy. They had the eternal hope of immortality, of becoming persons in the heavenly abode.

Finally, a strong and plausible explanation for the appeal of early Christianity to women can be made on the grounds that even while its symbols were overtly masculine and its faith centered directly on a historical male figure who had ascended from among the dead, it had preserved a certain, unmistakable character that embodied the feminine side of religious life. This feminine dimension can be traced all the way back to the styles of worship in Israel during the first millennium B.C.E.

The realization that God has a feminine side apparently occurred to ancient peoples whom we would routinely describe as patriarchal. This type of data, on the other hand, has been largely overlooked by many feminist scholars because of their tendency to concentrate on the social status of women, which was universally inferior among all peoples of the Iron Age, when the Bible was composed. The sociological fallacy, therefore, has diverted a good deal of attention away from the real possibilities for both faith and worship that are embedded, like wealthy veins of precious metal, *within the tradition itself.*

Male and Female Faces of God

What we find, ironically, through a linguistic and ideological analysis of much biblical literature is that despite both ancient and modern wording, *the God of Israel is an "engendering" Deity who is revealed in both male and female guises.*

The idea of a God that is disclosed exclusively in terms of gender must strike us somehow as a little hard to swallow. But we must remember that classical theology always allowed God the prerogative of self-revelation in whatever ways were appropriate to the historical situation. The notion advanced at times by both traditionalists and fundamentalists that there are certain inalterable concepts or figurations to represent the Godhead—and that these signifiers happen to be male—is not only idolatrous, it is quite unbiblical, if not blasphemous.

Indeed, if we may be quite blunt, there is really no basis in either scripture itself, or what might be called the reformed perspective on the tradition, to support any kind of assertion that God is specifically male. The very rule of divine transcendence will not allow it. If the rule of transcendence logically implies a God who could manifest as both male and female, is it then not reasonable to presuppose that the divine has, in fact, been exhibited under both aspects?

The issue of what the feminine side of God really means, on the other hand, has been clouded in the past generation by archaeological discoveries and religious speculation concerning archaic goddess worship.

The thesis first propounded in the late nineteenth century that prior to the growth of civilization there existed some form of worldwide veneration of a mother-goddess figure has now been generally accepted by scholars of religion. The persistence of this cult of the *Magna Mater* until as late as the Middle Ages in some cultures has also been supported by a significant body of research.

As historical and anthropological findings have accumulated, the theoretical debates have tended to focus on the degree to which goddess religion may have been a universal faith of prehistoric humanity, much like Buddhism, or Islam, or Christianity. Some feminist scholars have seized on the new research and argued that goddess religion, in view of its antiquity, should be regarded as a real and powerful contemporary alternative to Judaism or Christianity.

Promoters of goddess religion have gone so far as to make the claim that the prevalence of this type of worship in the distant past is clear evidence of a time when women were highly honored, if not actually accorded greater prestige than men. Actual experimentation with such an alternative has been going on for quite some time, especially in such places as California, under the banner of what has come to be called neopaganism.

While critics of the goddess renaissance have been quick to point out that sweeping conclusions about an exalted status for women in the

Stone Age cannot be drawn from the meager material available, a major problem lies with the present-day sorts of spirituality that such a revival might imply.

Ancient goddess religion was not exactly a peaceful and happy affair, as ancient writers who observed its practices have attested, and as anyone might also infer from its survival among preliterate peoples. There are definite indications that such religion, when practiced, often involved violence and mutilation, not to mention bloody sacrifice.

These practices are, of course, not found today among the various neopagans, who claim the ancient symbol systems as their own and who honestly maintain that they are upholding as high an ethical standard, if not a higher one, than the Christian church itself has permitted over the years. But anthropological perspectives, such as those of the famous French researcher René Girard, make it evident that so much of ancient paganism, at least, relied on ritualized violence as a means of social control and the assurance of religious ecstasy.[2]

Such demurrals, of course, should not serve to locate goddess worship on a lower rung of the moral ladder than much of what has passed for high religion with its holy wars and its inquisitions. But they do restrain the belief that the second coming of such religiosity is not the lofty option that many feminists in their efforts to overcome the evils of the patriarchal era would claim.

Any reluctance in reinstating the great goddess to her throne in the twenty-first century does not stem from some male bias toward the mysteries of women. It has to do with the very focus of such a religion, which did not by any means in the archaic setting celebrate the divine feminine in its entirety. On the contrary, the ancient goddess religion simply *sacralized the turbulent life energies associated with birth, death, and sexual intercourse.*

That ancient goddess worship was intimately connected with fertility magic is beyond dispute. Most of the material artifacts, including clay figurines and cave inscriptions, that represent what today we would regard as the remains of the prehistoric goddess cult are connected with the miracle of new life and an erotic fascination with woman's body.

The headless little "Venus" statues of a female torso with pregnant belly dug up around Europe from the campsites of nomadic hunter-gatherers during the waning of the last Ice Age are stark evidence that the goddess faith was inseparable from the wonder and anxiety concerning conception and childbearing.

Yet this faith was also wrapped up with a mystique of the violent transformation of life that comes with ritual killing and the spilling of blood. In the prehistoric mind the magic of the menstrual blood that "brings forth" children and the shedding of blood during the hunt, supplying food to sustain the community as a whole, were symbolically and conceptually interlaced. The putative bloody rites of the ancient goddess religion, therefore, appear to have emerged from this fundamental psychology.

The performance of sacrifice was a basic metaphysical gesture in the face of the common experience that death—whether in the animal, vegetable, or human kingdom—always seems to eventuate in the reappearance of life, and that life can only be sustained through the violent transition into its opposite.

The religious controversies of remote antiquity, including the quarrel between the prophets of the Old Testament and the fertility cults that flourished in Palestine throughout the first millennium B.C.E., should not be interpreted principally as a struggle between matriarchy and patriarchy—terms that describe systems of social relations. They should be seen more as an argument over what is truly sacred.

It is time we recognized that the distaste of biblical Judaism for mother-goddess religion did not stem as much from misogyny as from its rejection of the primitive identification of the holy with the sanguinary and the organismic, an addictive psychology that in fact continues to lurk in the industries of prostitution and pornography and enslaves women to this day. The temple prostitutes that were the central fixtures of the matriarchal ceremonies of the ancient Mediterranean peoples may have been free from domineering husbands and male-centered family life, even while they were venerated by the society at large. But they certainly were no more prototypes of liberated women than the sex goddesses of the silver screen, such as Marilyn Monroe or Jayne Mansfield, have been in the twentieth century.

As social research gradually uncovers and pieces together the shreds and details pertaining to ancient religion, it may eventually come to the very simple conclusion that the reign of goddesses in olden days merely reflects at a psychological level the same kind of pedestal building and obsessive sexualization of women that feminists have always deplored.

The struggle between matriarchy and patriarchy may only have been a wrestling match for genital dominance with no more application to contemporary religious issues than debates over dietary laws. The hallmark of development for the historic religions of the world has been the emancipation of spirituality from the fetishism of genitality, even though this progressive trend admittedly has until recently contributed heavily to a more advanced form of misogyny that sees the female body as what the church fathers unashamedly described as the "Devil's gateway."

The signal triumph of modernity has been the acceptance of sexual behavior as a joyful and salutary form of human activity independent of the biological necessity of procreation. But this triumph, which has proceeded apace with the movement toward social equality for women, has not been matched with any powerful and coherent realignment of underlying religious attitudes and symbols to express what is obviously a new appreciation of the divine order of things.

Goddesses are exactly what such a polytheistically slanted term suggests: *fragments of a much larger, still unthought and undiscovered, spiritual whole that is larger than the simple term "female."* Thus the search for a religious and theological framework in which not only women but also men can feel at home nowadays in relation to their significant others must go beyond all efforts to dredge up outdated and barely usable models from the forgotten past.

The search must turn on an understanding of the fundamental difference between simple sexuality and gender as a way to approach the problem of men and women in the fabric of the cosmos.

For a long while such an approach was hampered by the dogma of social scientists during the last generation that one cannot speak of any measurable difference between men and women, other than with respect to genes and anatomy. This dogma, in turn, had been fueled by a reaction to the social conservatism of the same profession during the previous generation which maintained that, as Sigmund Freud put it, "anatomy is destiny."

What is happening now in clinical inquiry, however, is the realization that men and women may be "wired" somehow physiologically and cerebrally to experience the world differently, but that these different dispositions have virtually nothing to do with political capabilities and social authority. The upshot is that it has become permissible finally to regard male and female differences as part of the fruitful balance of all creation, and that we can begin to talk about a man-woman "spirituality" as if it were something much more profound than a religious means of acting out what are at the core nothing more than social roles.

The Engendering Godhead

The concept of gender, which has begun in both social and academic discourse to replace the notion of sex in both social-scientific and theological discussions of males and females, itself connotes a more complex set of issues.

"Sexuality" means a specific kind of biological differentiation. "Gender" suggests an overriding distinction in the human quality of experience, which can be shared by people irrespective of their bodily makeup, even though, for example, a feminine orientation is naturally associated with the bodies of women.

For obvious reasons it becomes intellectually difficult, if not logically impossible, to speak about the sex of God, whereas the thought that the divine has gender is no more outlandish than the assignment of such attributes to inanimate objects in the majority of the world's languages. Indeed, the fact that the grammars of these languages themselves tend to ascribe gender to all objects they name may reveal something about what informs human experience at its most rudimentary levels.

Finally, when we begin to think of the divine as in certain circumstances having gender, we are compelled to discard the notion that God is either exclusively male or female, and we can become gradually comfortable with the proposition that he or she can be *both* masculine and feminine, depending on the context of experience.

When we move to a broader theological plane of reflection, we may even have to speak of an engendering Godhead, and perhaps even a gendered gospel in accordance with which people may make a profession of faith. The theological notion of a self-gendering Godhead, on the other hand, has little in the absolute sense to do with the social functions of men and women, even though it clearly implies equality between men and women in every respect.

The idea of an engendering Godhead is closely bound up with the effort to grasp the searching and abiding meaning of the well-known saying in Genesis, "in the image of God [God] created [humankind]; male and female [God] created *them*" (Gen. 1:27, italics added).

The theme of an engendering Godhead has oversize implications for the present-day religious situation. The great theological escarpment of the twentieth century, which few thinkers have been able to scale successfully, is the notion of a *personal God*. While the personality of the Godhead has been a staple in the language of faith among traditional believers, it has been chronically difficult either to affirm or to explain theologically.

The problem of giving some rational account of the traditional creedal assertion of divine personhood has been compounded by the assaults of twentieth-century philosophy on the metaphysical architecture in which such a concept originally had pride of place. The doctrine of God as a supreme will and agency has been rendered intellectually confusing in a climate of extreme suspicion about monotheism and in a secular culture favoring social scientific paradigms of religious interpretation.

Yet to raise the issue of gender in relationship to the divine decisively and unavoidably forces the question of divine personality to the fore. A gendered Godhead can be viewed as a useful, but not necessarily justifiable, pragmatic redesign of religious language to conform with cultural values and social expectations at the close of the millennium. In that respect such a concept is one more plotted point on the axis of rhetorical fashion within the history of liberal theology.

On the other hand, an engendering Godhead is a fuller and more radical kind of thought. It harks back to the challenging and almost paradoxical legacy of Christianity with its formulation that God is a unity behind several "persons."

Can we, or dare we, speak of God in a different and equally startling way as a unity behind what within the history of human life has always been regarded as the two ultimate "personal manifestations"? Can we say that God is *Two in One* as well as "three in one," as the classic Trinitarian doctrine maintains?

Can this confession of God's dyadic or binomial, as opposed to any sort of dualistic, nature be grounded in a radically new understanding of scripture and tradition itself?

The provocative statement of the author of Genesis has always been an implicit text for such a strategy of articulation. Indeed, the sense of God as Two in One—when the binomial formula refers not to some internal opposition but to the complementarity of gender—is no contemporary social construction of reality.

It is not merely some tacit strategy to bring the grammar of theology up-to-date in keeping with new day-to-day relationships between men and women. It is a millennial disclosure of what God has always meant to be from God's own standpoint. And the hint of this divine intention can be discerned from a rereading of the very sources of faith itself.

Gnosticism

The idea of the Two in One, therefore, rests critically on what has always been considered in different ways and at different moments in history the Christian understanding of God's character and purpose. Most theological efforts in the past twenty years to sketch a feminine face for divinity have wandered not just off the main roads of tradition, but into narrow byways and rutted lanes, sometimes arriving even at dead ends.

Writers such as Elaine Pagels have raised much dust by claiming to have found an alternative to what she considers the misogyny of the old Christian orthodoxy in the Gnostic gospels of the first centuries.[3] The Gnostics were a shadowy but highly influential group of early Christian heretics who denied such articles of faith as God having died on the cross or the catholic community of all believers.

The Gnostics held that Jesus was but the physical apparition of a remote and wholly spiritual cosmic entity, who came not to save human beings from sin but to teach a powerful, mysterious, and altogether secret form of knowledge about the universe. The word for "secret knowledge" in Greek is *gnosis* (hence, Gnostic).

Pagels's work, which has been criticized by some scholars as excessively speculative, contends among other things that this secret knowledge was considered heretical, because it gave strong weight to the feminine cast of religious experience. The suggestion has been drawn by her defenders that if the Gnostic perspective had somehow won out over the orthodox one, the subordination of women to men in the teachings of the Christian church would not have emerged so clearly.

The trouble with this line of argument, however, is that it tries to make a more whole theological cloth out of ancient Gnosticism than the surviving texts of that particular legacy warrant.

There is no question that Gnosticism allowed for a feminine voice in its liturgies with an aggressiveness that conventional Christianity did not.

There is also little doubt that the Gnostics intuitively saw that true Godhead must be both male and female, and they sometimes expressed this sentiment by talking about the androgynous nature of divinity. Yet

Gnostic instruction did not contain anything sharp or coherent enough to pass muster as what Pagels calls a gospel.

Gnostic feminism, if one reads its different texts and fragments carefully, was a somewhat undirected effort to incorporate and furnish some form of intellectual rendering of the numerous myths and symbolic patterns of the ancient world involving goddesses. Ancient Gnosticism, in fact, has often been called the New Age Movement of its own age, for it was a veritable potpourri of exotic religious enthusiasms and experiments.

Thus it is not too difficult to conjecture how Gnosticism did, in fact, draw on certain strands of the religious imagination rejected by mainline theologies. The trouble is that these religious forms are for the most part unintelligible to contemporary persons. Moreover, they were considered far beyond the comprehension of the masses even in their own day.

Today a Gnostic gospel can no more be expected to deal successfully with the religious displacement of women in an era of gender equality than a reinstatement of the old, bloody altars of the neolithic matriarchy. Authentic religious revolutions do not depend on the importation of foreign and unfamiliar practices and ideas. They occur when the sparks of a radical new comprehension of existing tradition have been smoldering for some time within the tinder of social upheaval and intellectual malaise.

Any serious rethinking, or even a rewriting, of the Jewish-Christian past cannot proceed by simply dismissing it out of hand as patriarchal. Nor can it be advanced by recurrence to arcane belief systems that can only be made palatable by a religious romance of the goddess invented in the twentieth century, or by bowdlerizing the very passions and violence that gave energy to goddess worship during its historic lifetime.

The question remains: Is it possible to read deeply back into the tradition itself to recover what has yet been unspoken or hidden, what was always there but somehow hardly recognized, what was never intended to be happenstantial or marginal, yet became so because of the peculiar patriarchal epoch in which it was buried or covered over?

Is it possible now to *think theologically* in such a way that we can ascertain the feminine half of God in a "style of dress" that is just as compelling and, strangely, as familiar as the "God of our fathers"? Can such an archaeology of the divine feminine uncover the same contents as what classically has been regarded the heart of biblical revelation?

The Bible and Sophia

A project to disclose what we have in mind by the engendering Godhead must begin with the essential source of the tradition itself—the Bible.

At first glance, any attempt to achieve such an objective by going back into the Bible itself would seem as formidable as trying to scale Mount

Everest. Not only is the summit craggy, remote, and at cloud-wrapped heights above terrifying and giddy precipices, the path to the top itself is fraught with obstacles, dangers, and the lengthening shadows of the impossible.

On a practical level, one must also face up to the fact that the Bible is rarely "read" anymore with a clear mind and an open heart to detect new glimmerings of insight and vistas of meaning. What the ponderous armor of fundamentalism has not stifled and let wither, the increasingly ideological social and historical study of the Bible has choked with its tendency to reduce the richness of the text to a set of externalities and irrelevancies. According to these perspectives, the Bible is either the Word of God and a thesaurus of Christian truths and values that are eminently culture-bound, or it is a mystifying political document that can be dismissed on a variety of half-critical counts.

In addition, any rescue mission to regain the still-concealed kernel of the tradition must involve recourse to what we would term a venture into *biblical theology*. The concept of biblical theology is increasingly problematic in the era of extensive, exact, and often conflicting scholarship regarding every jot and genre of the scriptural canon.

Some might argue that thinking about the Bible theologically was only possible in a more innocent era when the range of interpretative agendas was not as great as today, or when the correlation between a proper understanding of the text and the openness of faith was taken for granted. It is certainly foolish to develop any kind of systematic theological perspective from the study of a book that has been classically viewed as a series of testaments to mysterious divine actions in a welter of dimly remembered circumstances at the fringes of recorded history and communicated through commandments, oracles, apothegms, and narratives.

Our aim, however, is not the accomplishment of any straightforward theological mission. Nor is it precisely a feminist reading of the biblical texts, which has usually fostered a suspicion about the role and importance of the texts themselves. The purpose is simply to discover meanings buried within the language of the tradition itself.

In the ancient world this way of going about things was known as the quest for wisdom. The quest today is virtually the same. And it is the so-called wisdom tradition itself, which forms such an important segment of the biblical canon, that shall be beacon to guide us, and the source of our inspiration.

The relationship between the heritage of biblical revelation and the wisdom tradition has long been ignored, particularly throughout much of the Protestant era. The search for wisdom at the heart of the scriptures, however, was always the key strategy of exegesis in the ancient world, and such an imperative can be found at the core of biblical injunctions.

if you take my words to heart
and lay up my commands in your mind,
giving your attention to wisdom
and your mind to understanding,
if you summon discernment to your aid
and invoke understanding,
if you seek her out like silver
and dig for her like buried treasure,
then you will understand the fear of the LORD
and attain to the knowledge of God;
for the LORD bestows wisdom
and teaches knowledge and understanding.
(Prov. 2:1–6)

God gives of "herself" and gives us wisdom of the knowledge and understanding of the feminine side of Godhead. This delving into the springs of wisdom is itself the proper response of faith to the majesty of the divine. The attainment of wisdom is part of the process of glorification that comes from fulfillment of the purpose for which human beings were created.

The glory of God is to keep things hidden
but the glory of kings is to fathom them.
(Prov. 25:2)

As the first quotation makes apparent, the striving after wisdom is also a reaching toward the *divine feminine*. Wisdom is always a female personification in the Bible, and as we shall see in subsequent chapters, is far more than a suggestive metaphor.

The feminine figure of Wisdom looms larger than scholars have previously realized in the Jewish scriptures, and even more so in the New Testament. As recent research has pointed out, she is a complex theological derivative of both traditional Hebrew characterizations of Deity and representations of feminine divinity throughout the Mediterranean cultures of antiquity.[4]

Wisdom is not the goddess so much as she is the feminine engendering of Godhead. She is the side of God that draws close, becomes intimate, and unites with human beings. She is frequently associated with prophetic authority and special inspirations given to those who are given a sudden glimpse of the unsearchable, divine purpose.[5]

The old goddess cults of Palestine dwelt upon the distinctly erotic and procreative aspects of the divine feminine, thereby separating the magical attributes of womanhood from the broader humanistic consensus about what gods are, and what divinity means, that emerged in Greco-Roman times.

But the tradition surrounding this figure called Sophia in the Greek Old Testament—like the worship of the male presence addressed as Yahweh in the Hebrew temples—arose out of a long-term process, whereby the passionate and willful masks of the holy gradually absorbed into an ethical personality for the divine. This ethical personality became the cornerstone of both rabbinic Judaism and early Christianity.

Sophia and Christian Tradition

There are always strong echoes of Sophia's sexuality in the Old Testament, even what might be described as her erotic sportiveness. She is sometimes a woman of the streets, sometimes a seductive bride. She is obviously a beautiful, alluring, and commanding woman. But she is also a treasure trove of divine secrets.

She is God's "hidden riches," which may be taken to mean that she is revealed by patient courting and attending, by entering into an ever-deepening "relationship" with the one who seeks after her. Nothing about her can be considered transparent or obvious, a fact that should not be ignored by fundamentalists. Just as wisdom in the philosophical sense implies the exploration of the depths of our surface understanding of language and the world, so Sophia at the theological level reflects what the human mind and heart is yearning to know about the fathomless Godhead.

Sophia is what the medieval mystics called the *Deus absconditus,* the "concealed God." Sophia is the signifier "W" in both earth and in heaven. She is what is meant most fully by the term "woman."

The realization that the science—what the Romans called *sapientia,* "wisdom"—of God is the *search for Sophia* has startling implications for religious thought in the twentieth century. In a somewhat trite sense it implies that theology must become not anthropology, but *philo-sophy,* the "love of Sophia."

But it also points to a way of confronting the enormous challenge of properly engendering religious speech and thought. A reaching back into the sources of the tradition for the underground treasure of wisdom gives impetus to any theological enterprise immersed in an archaeology of the feminine.

It is no mere patriarchal concession to a subordinate female element within the history of spirituality. It is truly "thinking the unthought" within the spectrum of Christian thought itself. It is a shattering disclosure of what really motivates and grounds the tradition—the Two in One.

The way of wisdom, as both ancient and modern myths tell us, is both the way up and the way down. The way of Sophia is the way to God through the sensual side of creation.

As the Lord God proclaims to the devil in the heavenly prologue of Goethe's *Faust,* the purpose of intelligent life is to descend into such depths that one comprehends the greatness of creation. Even the angels are rarely fit for the task. They shrink in terror from the top of the cliff when they behold the raging sea below.

The way of wisdom is the way of co-creation. It is to seek with divine help to master all possibilities, to actualize all talents, to confront everything and to fear nothing, to transform confused, sensate existence into forms and patterns that exude the divine glory.

The devil is cynical about such human prospects because, like any good Calvinist or Augustinian, he understands the wretchedness and pretentiousness of the fallen state. But with divine guidance the descent into the fallen world shall appear as the path of redemption. "Though now [humanity] serves me but confusedly," says the Lord, "I shall soon guide [them] toward what is clear."

In the end, the Lord proclaims:

> . . . may you
> Rejoice in beauty that is full and true!
> May that which is evolving and alive
> Encompass you in bonds that Love has
> wrought;
> And what exists in wavering semblance,
> strive
> To fix in final permanence of thought.[6]

The "beauty that is full and true" reminds us of the heavenly vision of Beatrice in Dante's *Divine Comedy*, or of Mary in Catholic devotional literature, or of Isis in the Egyptian religion. This vision has been captured mythically in the liturgies of Christianity, but it has not yet been completely and utterly thought as the other side of the wide tradition.

It is this investigation of the yet unchartered antipodes of Christian language and symbols that we shall here undertake in order to think through the fullness of Godhead.

We shall start at the beginning.

2
Old Testament and
Other Ancient Sources

Wisdom cries aloud in the open air,
she raises her voice in public places.—Prov. 1:20

Discovering the divine feminine at the core of Jewish-Christianity demands that we think more seriously about the way in which the language of scripture first arose.

For generations historians of Western religion have understood how the ancient Hebrews borrowed, adapted, and incorporated many of the forms of narrative and liturgy they found among the neighboring peoples of the ancient Near East, not to mention the very names used for God.

Biblical scholars, whether they will admit it or not, have always utilized some variation on what is otherwise known as the history of religions. The history of religions compares the beliefs, imagery, and structures of different religions to reckon how they have interacted with or influenced one another.

Many decades ago researchers found striking literary parallels between the biblical tales of both the Creation and the Flood and similar accounts etched on tablets from the moribund civilizations of Sumer and Babylon. And it is now clear that hymns of praise and service to the defunct deities of those peoples were restyled as words of worship for the Hebrew God Yahweh.

The theological view behind this kind of biblical historicism has been that the older Middle Eastern religions created the basic form for the sacred texts of the Hebrews. At the same time, the peculiar revelation ascribed to these texts supplied the content.

But this method of analysis has remained flawed in one crucial aspect. It fails to address why the authors and editors of the written tradition, which later coalesced as the Holy Bible, made the kind of literary choices they did. Indeed, much of the religion of the ancient Near East is wholly incompatible with the moral and spiritual values of the Bible. And the preponderance of the salvation history proper to the people of Israel, all the way from Adam through Abraham through the later kings of Judah, was as distinctive for the Hebrews as the gory epics of war gods were for the ancient Assyrians.

One might propose that there was always a universal dimension to ancient Near Eastern religion, and that the biblical writers drew, whenever appropriate, on these resources. But such a solution merely begs the question. The Hebrews did not arbitrarily pick certain religious ideas and themes from the surrounding cultures. On the contrary, they were deeply immersed in the struggles, passions, and contentions that contributed to the evolution of religious life in the first millennium B.C.E. around the Mediterranean basin.

The record that emerged as the Bible profoundly reflects this strife and stress. Yet the current generation of scholars acknowledges that the Bible is more an idealization of the travail of faith in the one, infinite God who is also Lord of history than a precise archaeological periscope that surveys the total scene from a privileged vantage point. The Bible is about faith, not about society. And all the efforts to reconstruct its meaning sociologically, or even ethnographically, must prove foolish and fruitless, since the data to make sense out of the text at that level are actually quite scant.

God

By the same token, the current fashion of talking about the sex of God, or imposing what are clearly contemporary psychological or political categories on the vastness of a spiritual legacy, is not as easy as it may seem at first. Anthropological analysis can prove quite instructive for illumining the context of everyday life. It may even tell us something we obviously know from sources outside the Bible—that females in the ancient world, for instance, had few rights on earth if not in heaven, and that the unshakable authority of these ancient texts has prevented the emancipation of women spiritually, even while they have been liberated socially and culturally. But it does little to resolve the issue of how the divine itself in Jewish-Christianity can be said to have become identified with the male gender.

The shortcoming of biblical historicism, even that which concentrates on the oppression of women as the social milieu within which the Bible was composed, is that it avoids dealing with the dynamics of the development of the biblical symbols themselves. Ordinary people in the High Middle Ages did not build Gothic cathedrals simply to disclose the poverty of their daily lives, or to offer a canny camouflage for feudal hierarchy. The same process would have occurred centuries earlier during the Dark Ages, if social oppression had been the motivating factor. But it did not.

The age of cathedrals was an effort at finding an architecture that would express the new imagination of faith. This imagination of faith, in turn, was propelled through improved literacy, the growth of learning, and a rising mercantile economy that depended on ambitious business ventures and foreign commerce. Likewise, the writing of the Bible managed to codify the self-knowledge of an ancient aggregation of nomadic tribes, whose heritage was not determined solely by war and conquest, but by an ideal of religious unity that was summed up in the phrase "the people of Israel."

Israel, in fact, was never so much a place-name as what we would call an *eschatological* reality. The word "eschatology" derives from the Greek *eschaton*, which means the "end of things." The early Hebrews, like the Christians who came after them, were always directed in their doctrines and thinking toward the conclusion of world events. Not all Hebrew thought, of course, was eschatological.

Israel was the name that underscored the coalescence of tumultuous, and often confused, historical happenings into a divine purpose. It was always the failure of political aims and the breakdown of social order in the Hebrew commonwealth that led to the prophetic sense of a higher, and more inscrutable, pattern of God's activity in the world. The Bible is not a history book, nor is it simply a "guide to living." It is, as the very nomenclature for its sections implies, a series of testaments to the workings of the divine, which usually are not at all intelligible from an everyday vantage point.

A question arises, therefore, as to the meaning of biblical language, which obviously implies the concrete power and presence of God, and whether this language can be considered normative in any sense. The question becomes especially acute when it applies to the language of gender, inasmuch as most God-talk in the Bible has in fact been sanctified by the prevalence of the masculine gender.

The theological charges and countercharges that have framed the problem in recent years have been driven, ironically, by a misapprehension of the grammar of God in the Bible. These theological wrangles have been predicated on the false premise that words about God can be analyzed in accordance with conventional theories of semantics. The assumption has been that the technical canons of reference, metaphor, connotation, and analogy suffice somehow to clarify the text. Even from the standpoint of biblical archaeology, it is obvious that the Bible was never intended as a linguistic object to be dissected and sociologically reduced to a most common denominator. As Klaas Smelik has noted, the Bible was always meant to be read aloud, and "whenever we now read the Bible silently to ourselves with the same haste as we read a newspaper, we miss a lot. The Bible was not intended for that kind of consumption."[1]

Much contemporary controversy about the Bible misses the point that words about God in the Bible are always part of the language of response to the divine self-disclosure. Furthermore, this self-disclosure cannot be conditioned or limited by the fact of gender. One does not name the God of the Bible. The name is always given. To impose such a limitation on God constitutes idolatry, which theologians on the right and on the left regularly commit.

Indeed, a careful reading of the way in which the divine title functions in biblical worship suggests that the ultimate name of God is always given under the aspect of the given names of the Most High for that period and culture. We can discern this process when Moses meets God for the first time on the mountain in the book of Exodus. God first introduces himself as the God of the fathers, the God of Abraham, Isaac, and Jacob, thus observing the conventions of a patriarchal culture.

But God's grand disclosure at this instant in what theologians would call revelation history also shatters the mold of linguistic custom within the patriarchy. If God is the God of "the fathers," such a God is also Yahweh, the "I AM WHO I AM," the name beyond names.

In the moment of biblical revelation there is always the association of the divine in terms of a recognizable mask. But there is also a tearing away of the mask and an encounter with a divinity who is radically other. The self-revelation of the Deity invariably contains within itself the intimation of a *Deus absconditus,* a "hidden God" who is indecipherable with respect to the expectations of a particular time or culture.

We witness this event, which we may call the inversion of the signs of the divine. This inversion is very much in evidence in the New Testament, both in the Gospels and in the writings of Paul.

Asherah and Sophia

In the Synoptic Gospels, we meet Jesus the Rabbi, whom many suspect is the Messiah, but remain exceedingly doubtful because he does not at all fit the familiar profile. This profile is first fractured by the tragedy of the crucifixion, then turned on its head with the incidents of Easter morning. The inversion is the key to the biblical drama itself. Moreover, the inversion occurs in an even more radical manner through the significations of gender.

While it is indisputable that the masculine voice prevails throughout the Old Testament, there are undeniable inklings as well of what some writers have called the "hidden goddess" in the same passages. The term "Hebrew goddess," of course, may be a misnomer. It was coined by a contemporary Jewish scholar named Raphael Patai, author of an important but controversial book titled *The Hebrew Goddess,* first published in 1967.

Patai claims to have found throughout the inscriptions and archaeological remains of ancient Israelite civilization the persistence of "feminine numina" that were manifestly "part of the Hebrew-Jewish religion, whether they were admitted into the 'official' formulation of the faith, or accepted only by the simple people, against whose beliefs and practices the exponents of the former never ceased to thunder."[2]

Patai's interpretation relies on the reasonable historical inference that, because the prophets of Israel railed against the adoption of local "goddess cults" by their people, the religious motive behind these beliefs and practices that were so common in Canaan must have burrowed into the Hebrew faith itself. Patai has endeavored to show how this sensibility had more of an impact on biblical tradition than has been suspected.

Patai begins with the divine figure of Asherah, "the earliest female deity known to have been worshipped by the Children of Israel."[3] He cites various references in the book of Kings where prophets of Israel, such as Ahijah, condemn the rulers of Israel for setting up graven or molten images to Asherah. Ahijah attributes the breakup and division of the kingdom of Israel to Solomon's importation of alien forms of worship, including Asherah. Finally, it was the actual, formal introduction of Asherah devotion into the royal house of Israel by King Ahab in the ninth century B.C.E. that spurred the celebrated confrontation between the monarch and the prophet Elijah.

Ahab had married Jezebel, daughter of Ethbaal, king of Sidon. Sidon was the center of Asherah worship. Elijah attacked the idolatrous practices of Ahab, which included erecting altars to the fertility god Baal, as well as to Asherah. He set about to prove who truly was "God in Israel." He arranged for a public rainmaking contest atop Mount Carmel, in which Yahweh miraculously intervened with a bolt of lightning to demonstrate cosmic power (1 Kings 18:17–40).

Despite Elijah's victory on behalf of Yahwism, the biblical authors are none too bashful in reporting that veneration of Asherah continued for successive generations. Other research has led to the same conclusions drawn by Patai. The prophetic denunciation of idolatry may have gone more against the average religious practices of the day than has been fancied until now.

There is, for example, the famous altercation between the prophet Jeremiah and the women of Jerusalem over the practice of making "crescent-cakes" and burning them as sacrifices to the "queen of heaven." The Queen of Heaven was a Palestinian fertility goddess, who may have been either Ishtar or Asherah.[4] Jeremiah blames Judah's coming destruction at the hands of the Chaldean armies on this type of worship.

But the Jewish women insist that the practice, going back generations, guaranteed the prosperity of the nation, and that its abandonment would be the true cause of calamity. The women proclaim that they have made "promises" and have sworn fealty to "her" rather than the male Yahweh. In other words, the controversy of faith referenced in Jeremiah was over whether it was loyalty to Yahweh, or an implicit covenant with the Queen of Heaven, that ensured salvation.[5]

Patai shows how the divine feminine as an oppositional force in the prophetic literature gradually is changed into a complementary power in later Judaism. He documents how the various and complex kinds of feminine numina that appear in the Bible, or in traditions related to the Bible, can be viewed in later periods of biblical history as independent agencies which, even if they are brought "into conflict with God," manifest "their own, different, but equally valid will to good."[6]

Patai points, for example, to the concept of the divine Shekinah, or "glory" of God, which literally means "act of dwelling." In later Judaism the ancient Hebrew notion of God's real and concrete presence, experienced as a "cloud" filling the sanctuary, became the Shekinah—a female personality who performs a nurturing and maternal role in relationship to the wayward children of Israel.

The figure of the Shekinah also bears close analogy to the later, and very important, idea of personified Wisdom—*Hokhma* in Hebrew, *Sophia* in Greek.

The divine character of Sophia decidedly influenced the religious outlook of early Christianity and becomes the key to an appreciation today of the equality of males and females, both here and in the beyond. Indeed, so much of the Christian understanding of what is meant by "God incarnate" had its mythic and intellectual origins in the Hebrew tradition of the divine feminine.

The problem with Patai's research, unfortunately, is that it provides no coherent theory of how the fertility "goddesses," against whom the prophets inveighed at the beginning of the first millennium B.C.E., were kin to the more lofty conception of Sophia as Yahweh's feminine companion, which gained acceptance during the period starting about 500 B.C.E., or just when Israel fell under the imperial boot of Persia, Macedonian Greece, and finally Rome.

An obvious explanation, offered in the twentieth century by depth psychologists such as Carl Jung, is that the female half of God, rejected by the early patriarchal cult of Yahweh, came gradually to be integrated into both the collective mind-set and theological framework of the Hebrew people.

But this version of what took place over many centuries is far too simplistic. The significance of Patai's work has been its recognition that the unofficial religion of the Bible has always made room for the richness and subtlety of feminine experience. Both Judaism, and by extension Christianity, have accommodated from the beginning the female perspective far more readily than what we would expect of the Western religious canon.

Yet the suggestion that these noncanonical traditions inherently relied on goddess worship as an alternative to the rigidities of patriarchal culture falsifies the underlying historical mechanisms that have been at work. The fundamental issue in ancient times was never male versus female so much as the hegemony of the heavenly versus the corruptions of the earthly. The cults of the divine feminine in ancient Canaan were intimately enmeshed with the practice of sex magic, which held very little moral regard for women, despite the romantic rewriting of religious history under way today.

The prophetic rhetoric that condemned Asherah worship as whoring or prostitution was not simply a polemical strategy for demeaning women. It referred to the way in which ceremonial magic, used primarily for the benefit of agriculture throughout the settled zones of Palestine, undermined the traditional Hebraic sense of God's transcendence while corroding the social fabric.

We need to remember that actual prophetic denunciations of the goddesses had little to do on the surface with the fact that they were women. Almost uniformly, these tirades centered on social injustice and mistreatment of the less fortunate, which often accompanied such religious practices.

The emergence of a sense in later biblical times that God is gendered and can be predicated as both male and female belongs within the logic of the tradition itself. In addition, the evolution of that perspective has critical implications for how we utilize the tradition nowadays. As Anne Baring and Jules Cashford point out, throughout the wisdom literature of the Bible in which the exalted language of the divine feminine recurs consistently, "She"

> is the feminine counterpart of the masculine deity, the foundation of the world, the master-craftswoman. She speaks both as the unifying light, which is the ground of creation, and the form that "clothes" it. She is the hidden law that orders it. She describes herself in language that shows that she is the animating power in nature and human life: rooted in tree, vine, earth and water as well as in the human creation of the city. She is judge . . . and saviour . . . interceding to save her people, as Ishtar interceded to save humanity from the Flood. She is transcendent, eternally one with the godhead beyond creation, and immanent in the world as the presence of the divine within the forms of creation. She is the invisible spirit guiding human life, who may be discovered by the person who seeks her guidance and help.[7]

Baring and Cashford also observe that the biblical myth of incarnate Wisdom is in some sense a revival of older motifs that the religious conventions surrounding the worship of Yahweh had excluded. In its battle with Canaanite fertility magic the priesthood of Yahwism cast aside a universal and more diffuse religious conception of the depths of divine existence.

In prehistoric times this conception had been mythically expressed as the "body" of the Mother Goddess. The feeling that the earth with its cycles of life and death was sacred in its own right lurked behind the tendency of the religious imagination to make a distinction between gods and goddesses. The ongoing conflict between the two spheres of worship—the infinite sky from which the life-giving rain fell and the dark ground out of which vital existence itself arose—fostered an ancient clash, which has been interpreted too facilely as a gender war within religion.

It should be noted that much adoration of the goddess across the span of religious history has focused on the iconography of the male phallus, not the female genitals. The split has actually been between conferring supreme value on the physical body and its sexual energies and the worship of something much higher.

Ironically, what we find in the Old Testament is not so much a rejection of earth-based religiosity as its absorption into the vision of Yahweh. These traditions constitute the backdrop to the wisdom books and serve to raise the notion of the divine feminine from the sacred sensuality of the fertility cults to an ethicospiritual ideal of the compassionate, loving, ever-faithful better half of God's nature.

The Wisdom Tradition
in the Bible

It is the *wisdom literature,* occupying a sizable space within the biblical canon, that has not been properly mined for these treasures of the spirit and for the intellectual ore that can be refined into genuine theological thinking about the divine feminine.

It is more than a historical curiosity that the wisdom tradition in ancient Judaism has been securely identified with the life and teachings of King Solomon. Strangely, it is the same King Solomon whom the prophetic tradition held in not-too-thinly disguised contempt for having trafficked in idolatry and introducing foreign gods, particularly Asherah, into Israel.

Solomon, in contrast with other patriarchal heroes of the faith, was remembered as a "lover of women" (1 Kings 11:1). He was best noted for his meeting with the mysterious Queen of Sheba, who came with her retinue to "test him with hard questions" and to challenge his fame as a minion of wisdom (1 Kings 10:1ff.).

The story from Kings suggests that the Queen of Sheba may have been a competitor in the venerable craft of "the wise," which in many cultures has been revered as the fountainhead of philosophy and the wellspring of culture and education. In the book of Kings, Solomon's gifts of "wisdom" are seen as indispensable to maintaining the "prosperity" of the nation. But the legend of the Queen of Sheba evidently attests to an underlying affiliation between the cult of wisdom and a higher status for women than the rural patriarchy of Israel in previous generations had permitted.

Mythological surveys of the figure of Wisdom in the ancient world have uncovered a definite Egyptian connection.[8] Wisdom is regarded as sister to the Egyptian goddess Maat. Maat, in turn, is associated with the fecundity of the land carried by the Nile and with the social harmony resulting from the administration of law and justice. Later on Maat became the same "Great Goddess" of that country, known as Isis.

The wisdom books of the Bible consistently exhibit Egyptian literary influence. Given the adversarial character of the Egyptians in traditional Judaism through the legends of Moses and the exodus, this tendency seems a little odd, if not paradoxical.

Moreover, early Christianity seemed to have a different take on the land of Egypt. Unlike the children of Israel who fled Egypt just ahead of the menacing armies of Pharaoh, Jesus goes down with his mother, Mary, to Egypt to escape the persecution of Herod. It is as though Egypt were somehow Jesus' spiritual home. And it is not only the many apocryphal stories in early Christianity about Jesus' youthful studying and sojourning in Egypt that prompt this conclusion, it is also the myth of Christ as God's wisdom that we find in the writings of Paul and the Johannnine literature.

As we shall soon discover, the wisdom tradition becomes in the hands of the New Testament authors the very symbolic infrastructure of primitive Christianity. The relationship between the Old and the New Testaments, therefore, is wealthier and more complex than the traditional distinction of before and after Christ. As the power of the event of Easter morning confounded the early Christian community, they sought a more secure grasp of who Jesus was, why he had come, and what lay in the offing.

Even though biblical scholarship has exhaustively mapped the linkages and cross-references between the New Testament and the Jewish canon, the deeper reasons for the cleavage between the two faiths has never been satisfactorily addressed. The customary claim that Judaism, with its unnameable and radically "other" Deity, was inherently incapable of adapting to the Christian belief in a crucified God is less trenchant than meets the eye. Moreover, it ignores the fact that the opposition of the Sanhedrin and the rabbinate to the fledgling Christian sect was at its height *before* Christianity had clearly formulated its own anti-Jewish theological position. It also overlooks evidence of a hostility between the two camps prior to Jesus' trial and sentencing.

Early Christianity may have gathered both adherents and antagonists from the very start because it seemed to fulfill certain eschatological expectations within an important circle of Jews who were already at loggerheads with the establishment in Jerusalem. The popular view that early Christianity was some weird and marginal cult clustered around an obscure Galilean preacher, which happened to have become famous because of the tireless work and supreme promotional skills of one Saul of Tarsus, who later became Saint Paul, may require reassessment.

We know that the early church saw itself as the "true Israel." The important question is, Which Israel? Just as the venerable notion of a single Jewish tradition reflected in the narrative history and prophetic documents of what Christians term the Old Testament breaks apart on the shoals of an increasingly critical reading of the texts themselves and more scientific archaeology of the biblical environment, it becomes obvious that different opinons may have persisted all along about who were God's chosen people.

The well-known political split between the northern kingdom of Israel and the southern kingdom of Judah that took place right after the reign of Solomon during the late tenth century B.C.E. may hold clues to a deeper and more abiding theological rift at the heart of Hebraism.

The basis of the split is already rather familiar to biblical scholars. Its long-term and broader significance, however, has not been acknowledged, most likely because such a recognition flies in the face of more than a millennium and a half of patriarchal readings of the canonical texts. The key lies in the difference between the so-called Deuteronomic theology of history in the Old Testament and parallel versions of the same incidents written years after the Babylonian exile and contained in the books of Chronicles.

The Deuteronomic theology, which derives from the exaltation of the Mosaic Law expounded in the book of Deuteronomy, hinges on the commandment to Israel to remain faithful in worship to the one God who delivered it from captivity in Egypt. The theology is fairly simple. If Israel takes "care not to forget the LORD your God" and not to "fail to keep his commandments, laws, and statutes," the nation will prosper (Deut. 8:11–12). However, the divine voice proclaims: "If you forget the LORD your God and adhere to other gods, worshipping them and bowing down to them, I give you a solemn warning this day that you will certainly be destroyed" (Deut. 8:19).

Most of the history of Israel and its ruling families in the later centuries is contained in the books of Kings. Not surprisingly, it represents an attempt to apply the Deuteronomic formula to the actual course of events. Whenever Israel as a nation does well, according to the Deuteronomic writer, it is because the people served God loyally and did not stray toward any other forms of practice. But when Israel suffers hardship or ruin at the hands of its foreign enemies, it is because—as we find, for example, in the case of Rehoboam, Solomon's son, who was the target of the rebellion of the northern tribes—the people "did what was wrong in the eyes of the LORD, rousing his jealous indignation" by erecting "hill-shrines, sacred pillars, and sacred poles, on every high hill and under every spreading tree" as well as establishing cults of male prostitutes (1 Kings 14:22—24).

The image of Israel as a faithless woman who will not yield herself solely to her "husband" Yahweh, and who regularly suffers harsh punishment as an adulteress or whore, is striking throughout the Deuteronomic history. Even Solomon, David's son and successor, whom Jewish tradition reckons as one of the greatest, if not *the greatest,* of kings comes in for stern rebuke.

There is a murmuring throughout the Deuteronomic narrative of Solomon's reign that it was *he* who betrayed Israel, and who led it down the slippery slope toward dalliance with foreign gods. Finally, the Deuteronomist, the anonymous and hypothetical author of the books of Samuel and the books of Kings, concludes that this dalliance ultimately served as the cause of the nation's destruction at the hands of King Nebuchadnezzar of Babylon in the sixth century B.C.E. As the writer puts it, "Jerusalem and Judah so angered the LORD that in the end he banished them from his sight" (2 Kings 24:20).

Nevertheless, the corresponding tale of Solomon in 2 Chronicles is much more favorable and offers virtually nothing of the moral condemnation of Solomon's legacy, so prominent in Kings. Almost all attention falls on the dedication of the Jerusalem Temple and the glorification of Yahweh by providing for him a "dwelling" that will bear his "name."

Of course, Chronicles was composed by scribes during the time of Ezra and Nehemiah when the central task was the rebuilding of the Temple. Yet Chronicles has a significantly different message from that of the Deuteronomist. Whereas the Deuteronomist is preoccupied with the nation's moral behavior and its singular worship of Yahweh, the author of Chronicles zeroes in on God's promise to David that the Lord would have a "home" and that he would "tabernacle" with his people.

The high point of this passage is Solomon's prayer during the dedication of the Temple to the infinite God, which contains the theological rudiments that Christianity would later denote as the incarnation. The building of the Temple is the confirmation of God's word, which is effective regardless of the probity or the sinfulness of the people.

> But can God indeed dwell with man on the earth? Heaven itself, the highest heaven, cannot contain thee; how much less this house that I have built! Yet attend to the prayer and the supplication of thy servant, O LORD my God; listen to the cry and the prayer which thy servant utters before thee, that thine eyes may ever be upon this house day and night, this place of which thou didst say, "It shall receive my name." (2 Chron. 6:18–20)

The idea that the temple is a limited space for the presence, or dwelling, of the unlimited Godhead is doubtlessly a postexilic theme. But at the same time it casts into perspective what became perhaps a leading motif of postexilic Judaism—the need for a visible structure of signification for the godhead, an embodiment for the "name."

The act of dwelling corresponds to an appearance of the Shekinah, God's female side. The Shekinah is also called Wisdom by various pre-Christian and Jewish writers. The close identification between the ancient Hellenistic mythology of wisdom, personified as a powerful divine female personage who is frequently regarded as equal in stature with the masculine, and the Hebraic idea of the Shekinah, is the central clue to a still unwritten legacy of Jewish-Christianity, what might be dubbed its deep structure. It also explains why Palestinian Judaism split during the time of the Romans into the kingdom of Christianity, impelled by an apocalyptic enthusiasm among the devotees of the divine Sophia, and the kingdom of Mosaic legalists led by the Pharisees.

Shekinah

The formal religious concept of the Shekinah most likely has parallels in the writings of the great Jewish theologian Philo of Alexandria, whose reflections on the divine word and wisdom of God became an important impetus for later Christian thought. Philo was the first Jewish author to interpret the act of divine creation as having a sexual dimension. He is also the first to suggest that creation and procreation are intimately entwined with each other.

Philo says that the author of all things "was at the same time the father of what was thus born, whilst its mother was the knowledge possessed by its Maker. With His Knowledge God had union, not as men have it, and begot created things. And Knowledge, having received the divine seed, when her travail was consummated, bore the only beloved son who is apprehended by the senses, the world which we see."[9]

The language of a divine "son" who appears in the world as the visible image of God, of course, is the chief motif in early Christian literature, and its connection with the works of Philo is unmistakable. But the notion of God as engendering a sensible realm, or for that matter a concrete *imago*, would not have been possible in the ancient context without the prior recognition that the divine is in some mysterious sense female as well as male.

The intellectual development in classic Judaism that assimilated the idea of a female "personality" for the Godhead to the Old Testament theme of the Shekinah, or divine presence, was the confrontation with Platonism. The philosophy of Plato, which seeped into the Jewish centers of learning in the Egyptian city of Alexandria after the Macedonian conquest of the Near East in the fourth century B.C.E., stressed the duality of the cognitive mind and the senses.

In his academy in Athens, Plato had taught that *philo-sophy*, the love of wisdom, is grounded in the desire of the soul to free itself from the entanglements and confusion of sense knowledge and to soar toward the heavenly vision of truth, which is not clouded by bodily appetites, emotions, or everyday illusions.

On pagan soil this fundamental doctrine, which has suffused the cultural heritage of the West for thousands of years and has exerted an abiding influence on monastic Christianity, was responsible for much of the intrinsic misogyny of both Greco-Roman culture and the later Western church. For Platonic thought implicitly identified the realm of darkness and ignorance with sexuality and the female anatomy.

Greek philosophy had always been disparaging of serious man-woman relationships. And modern scholarship has shown convincingly the parallels between the Platonic ideal, as it was originally conceived, and male bonding.

Yet Platonic dualism was virtually alien to the integrative thought processes of the Hebrew sages. The natural response of a brilliant, Jewish philosopher such as Philo was to convert Platonic dualism into a theology of marital union between the two "faces" of God. This metaphysical solution conveniently corresponded with the orthodox view, enunciated in Genesis, that man and woman are the singular "image of God," and that they are "one flesh."

Philo himself did not talk specifically about a female Shekinah. Instead he elaborated on the conventional notion of Hokhma, or Wisdom.
But he may have very well understood the term "Shekinah," which takes
the feminine gender as an abstract noun in Hebrew and which he discerned as somehow cognate with the concept of *Hokhma* (Greek, *Sophia*),
to be the principle of God's affiliation, and enduring communion, with
the whole of creation.

The word "Shekinah" derives from the verb *shakhan,* which has the
basic meaning of "to dwell" or "to live with." While the feminine engendering of Shekinah in the Hebrew tongue seems to have had little
importance for biblical writers, the theological theme of God's "dwelling" with his people is immense in the Old as well as in the New Testament.

Solomon's construction of the Temple at Jerusalem was aimed at providing a permanent home for the infinite Godhead, for a sacred site
where the divine might forever dwell. In the larger picture the very notion of a Jewish temple depended on the realization that the supersensi-
ble must have a sensible embodiment, that the "I AM WHO I AM" must find
a way to show itself to humanity in time as well as space.

God's act of self-limitation is necessary to relate to the finite human
creature. But it is also indispensable to the act of creation. Rabbinic lore
tends to associate the intimacy of the Shekinah to her people with fidelity
and love for God. Whenever there is sin or violence in the world, the
Shekinah withdraws, and God is no longer said to "dwell" with the people.[10] When the people go into "exile" for their disloyalty, so does the
Shekinah.

Thus the destruction of the Temple at Jerusalem, which happened
twice in the history of the Jewish people, can be comprehended as having the monumental and devastating magnitude at which it was remembered for centuries. For the "end" of the Temple is also the withdrawal
of the divine presence, as it has been disclosed to the people all along.
In Judaic tradition the meshing of the symbols of Sophia, Shekinah, and
the Temple is not incidental, but helps us to decode finally the more
cryptic biblical messages that have survived, without having been fully
grasped, into the Christian epoch.

The fact that these symbols have distinct feminine overtones also en-
ables us to discern more clearly the meaning of the concealed tradition
within the conjoined chambers of both Judaism and Christianity. God is
engendered as female as well as male within the four dimensions of human experience, because the holy belongs to both the natural and supernatural realms, to history as well as eternity.

The puzzle behind the Christian belief in the miracle of divine incarnation resides in the mystery of the Two in One, of the engendering Godhead. *There can be no "Christian faith" in the most rudimentary, biblical sense
without an acceptance of the feminine half of God.* All theology of patriarchy,
whether it recognizes itself as such or not, is both incomplete and hereti-

cal in the way that such doctrines as Monophysitism, or Arianism, which stressed only the one side of the divine, were heretical. If it remains fixated on a male God it is even worse from an eschatological perspective. It is idolatrous, an abomination in the sight of the Most High.

The feminine half of God is the side that abides and sustains the human relation, that draws near and sheds love and forgiveness. It is the side that is made manifest in the unfolding of history. It is the side that shows the enormity of the divine presence, the reality of compassion and suffering, the silent struggle with faithlessness, violence, and evil. It is the side that waits to be revealed in the "fullness of time."

In Jewish thought the dwelling of the Shekinah and the descent of "wisdom" were apportioned to the time of fulfillment. Hence, the construction of the temple, where God would be at home and where wisdom in its profound depths would reign as it did in the period of Solomon and his glory, was always accorded a significance related to the end times.

Eschatology

It is no bare curiosity, therefore, that the so-called eschatological discourses of Jesus about the end of the world that occur in Matthew 24, Mark 13, and Luke 21 revolve around the destruction of the Temple at Jerusalem, and that it was Jesus' own sayings about dismantling the Temple that provoked his enemies to seek his torture and execution.[11]

What is clear, particularly if one examines closely the structure of the discourse and the context of the successive passages leading up to the story of Jesus' passion and resurrection, is that what scholars have called the eschatological crisis overshadowing the Synoptic Gospels betokens a radical shift in the biblical understanding of the divine dwelling or presence.

The "end of the age" to which Jesus alludes at the start of the discourse is marked by a tearing apart of the Temple. "Jesus was leaving the temple when his disciples came and pointed to the temple buildings. He answered, 'Yes, look at it all. I tell you this: not one stone will be left upon another; all will be thrown down'" (Matt. 24:1–2).

As the next passage indicates, the destruction of the Temple is closely linked with Jesus' "coming," his ultimate appearance, or *parousia*, conventionally but inappropriately translated as the "second coming." In fact, the historical narratives make it obvious that it is Jesus' entrance into the Temple, and his attempt to cleanse it by tossing out the money changers, which launches what the New Testament calls the final conflict.

The overt meaning of this particular "sign" is explained not in the Synoptic Gospels, but in the Gospel of John, which oddly seems to place the event early in Jesus' ministry.

> The Jews challenged Jesus: "What sign," they asked, "can you show as au-
> thority for your action?" "Destroy this temple," Jesus replied, "and in three
> days I will raise it again." They said, "It has taken forty-six years to build this
> temple. Are you going to raise it again in three days?" But the temple he
> was speaking of was his body. (John 2:18–21)

The destruction of the Temple as the divine dwelling place is the prelude to the transformation of all religious structures at the opening of
the new eon. It is the replacement of the architecture of stones with the
ingathering of the faithful in the "spirit," in the "body of Christ," which
would be called the church.

The historical toppling of the Temple at Jerusalem by the Romans in
70 C.E. confirmed this prophecy for the primitive Christians and spurred
the growth of the young sect. The dispute between Jesus and the Jewish
leaders of his day, which has always been somewhat murky for Christian
scholars, was not so much a question of messianic legitimacy.

Jesus' claims to the traditional messianic role as part of the House of
David, as we shall see, were never that strong and were not even encouraged among his followers. The dispute came down squarely on the role
and importance of the Temple for faith and worship.

One key to this interpretation can be found in Luke 19, where Jesus
makes his triumphal entry into Jerusalem. The pageantry described by
the Gospel writer recalls the victory march of a king, and the exaltation
of Jesus in verse 38 refers back to Psalm 118.[12] Yet, as a commentator in
a footnote in the *New English Bible* observes, Luke "has Jesus acclaimed as
king without mention of David."[13]

The orthodox belief would have required Jesus, if indeed he were the
returning Son of David, to be confirmed by the hallowing of his arrival
in Jerusalem and his enthronement at the Temple. But Jesus immediately denounces Jerusalem itself as failing to understand or lacking the
wisdom to decipher the reasons for these actions, which are indeed the
res gestae, "great deeds," of the king in his humble walk with the Most
High.

Furthermore, Jesus prophesies the end of the age of kings, cities, and
temples as the consequence of this failure and the beginning of a messianic kingdom that is no longer "of this world."

> When he came in sight of the city, he wept over it and said, "If only you had
> known, on this great day, the way that leads to peace! But no; it is hidden
> from your sight. For a time will come upon you, when your enemies will set
> up siege-works against you; they will encircle you and hem you in at every
> point; they will bring you to the ground, you and your children within your
> walls, and not leave you one stone standing on another, because you did
> not recognize God's moment when it came." (Luke 19:41–44)

God's "moment" is the New Presence in the person of Jesus. The eschatological signs of the closing of the age, therefore, betoken the replacement of the Temple as the location in time and space of the divine

Shekinah with the incarnate manifestation of God in human form. Jesus proclaims himself cryptically—as is common in the wisdom tradition—as the New Presence and as the embodiment, as Temple worship implied before him, of divine "wisdom."

One may hypothesize that it was not Jesus' alleged pretensions to the Davidic titles that upset the Pharisees and the Jerusalem priesthood. It was his proclamation of a new, yet at once very old, meaning for royal authority that may have always been at odds with the custodians of the Davidic, and hence the Deuteronomic, tradition.

This authority was vested in the power of Wisdom, and the mandate of the Shekinah. It was a power that was remembered by another group of traditionalists whose earlier sentimentality can be glimpsed in the legends of Chronicles. Because of their matriarchal sympathies, such traditionalists were far more popular with the common folk in the Judean countryside, the so-called *'am ha' arez,* "people of the land," than in the urban centers where the Davidic cult predominated.

While the Pharisees scorned Jesus and dismissed him as an impostor, the people recognized him immediately and responded to the coded messages he spoke, even in the parables. When Jesus entered the Temple, his actions signified the recapture of it by the guardians of wisdom, whose heroic archetype was King Solomon who had found a true dwelling place for the infinite God, and the ousting of the Pharisaic fetishists of the Law. It was Jesus' popularity with the people, which was understood but denied by the Pharisees, that comprised the eschatological confrontation.

Indeed, because of his popularity, as Luke tells us, the Pharisees could not prevent his teaching in the Temple and, even though they "were bent on making an end of him," they wound up "helpless, because the people all hung upon his words" (Luke 19:47–48). The Jewish masses were not unlike their counterparts in other countries that circled the eastern Mediterranean. What we find first during the Hellenistic period, and later under the Roman Empire, is a general decline in what historians and sociologists of religion have called rigorism, or legalism, and the flowering of various salvation cults that often revolve around a divine, maternal figure.

Isis

The most important of these maternal figures was the Egyptian goddess Isis, who performed much the same role in the earlier phases of Mediterranean paganism as Christianity did some centuries thereafter. As J. Gwyn Griffiths notes, the original Egyptian ideal of Isis expresses a "transcendent monotheism, the sense of one reality behind the many manifestations of polytheism."[14]

In fact, from a purely functional perspective Isis has striking similarities with Jesus. She offers unconditional love. She forgives sins. She is the gateway to a blissful eternity in the afterworld. Through her divinization is possible. She is called "the holy and eternal savior of the human race."[15]

The history of religions raises the tantalizing possibility that the pervasiveness of the Isis cult throughout the Roman Empire, and cloaked in different guises outside Egypt, may have laid the psychological foundations for the receptiveness of the Christian gospel. The maternalistic character of popular piety in the Mediterranean basin may have been a much more impelling factor in the spread of the teachings of the Nazarene than any interest in the Mosaic Law and its ethical precepts.

Church historians have always argued that as the Christian evangelists moved out of Palestine, they rapidly erased the Judaic coloring of the legends and beliefs concerning Jesus. But this familiar distinction may be overdrawn. In reality, the affinity between the Christ of the Gospels and the native maternal piety of the Gentiles may be stronger than scholars have admitted.

Jesus indeed may have been the charismatic minion of a strand of Jewish religiosity that was more inherently akin to Mediterranean paganism than the Davidic cult at Jerusalem. This strand was what we know in a broad way as the wisdom tradition.

Isis herself as "goddess of wisdom" was also the "mystic healer of the blind," curator of souls, and redeemer of the earth's wretched and lost. In this aspect, as Howard Clark Kee points out, she was "revered throughout the Graeco-Roman world and . . . her influence on both Judaism and the postexilic period and nascent Christianity is most readily apparent."[16]

The connections between the ceremonies of initiation into her mysteries, the acquisition of awesome and secret knowledge, healing, and the granting of life eternal are well documented.

Early Christianity required its own form of initiation—baptism—which was public, rather than secretive. But the mentality was by and large the same. According to a number of the so-called aretalogies, that is, tables of virtues and accomplishments that followers of Isis inscribed for posterity, the goddess loomed high above other female deities in the ancient world.

Isis was both the great culture bearer and lawgiver. She discovered the principles of agriculture and taught the arts of writing and navigation. She looked out for the welfare of mothers, children, and the family. The tradition taught that she was responsible for the attraction of the sexes to each other. She contrived marriage agreements and made sure that women were loved, and not abandoned, by their husbands. She kept the heavenly bodies in their orderly cycles.

But, most important, Isis was the "savior" of those who called on her from any place or in any predicament. Even the doctrine of "exclusivity," which has generally been construed as unique to Christianity, appears in the worship of Isis. Isis, like Jesus, was called "the only one." She was the inexchangeable portal to a secure and immortal existence.[17]

Although there is little evidence that devotion to Isis was causally related to the rise of Christianity, the formation of both traditions depended on virtually the same and historically contiguous collective factors. Moreover, ordinary scholarship misses the mark when it treats the texts and artifacts of Isis as though they were the remains of just one, more ancient, pagan goddess cult.

Isis worship absorbed many of the other cults, and was well on its way to becoming a universal faith that served as a spiritual backdrop to both Judaism and Christianity. It was not a singular entity that subsisted apart from the other great monotheistic religions.[18] It is rather more likely that Christianity itself can be viewed as the last wave of religious syncretism—the melding and combining of divergent symbols, actions, and beliefs—in the Mediterranean world.

Just as what was in the beginning an ethnically peculiar cult of the Nile goddess metamorphosized into a broad and democratic type of Hellenistic religiosity that changed the contours even of Judaism, so the new and far-flung diffusion of "savior piety" with its maternal appeal became *the chief ingredient in a synthesis with Hebrew monotheism that we know as the Christian faith.*

Religious historians are fond of focusing on clearly defined traditions with their corpora of authoritative writings, priestly hierarchies, and structures of command and control. This bias, which favors the study of masculine religious activity, has probably supplied more impetus to the idea that Christianity was a citadel of patriarchal teaching and practice than is completely accurate.

Increasingly advanced methods of historical analysis, however, show the ways in which the phenomenon of religion itself is both gossamer and fluid. What the populace holds dear and what the official hierarchies esteem are not always one and the same.

Early Christianity becomes far more intelligible when it is examined closely as part of the flux of Mediterranean popular culture.

3
From Eleusis to Early Christianity

[Sophia] is from the LORD;
[Sophia] is with him for ever.—Ecclus. 1:1

In addition to Isis, one of the most important manifestations of the divine feminine in ancient Mediterranean civilization was the Greek goddess Demeter. Demeter was the corn mother, the goddess of successful grain harvests and the fecundity of the earth.

In Greece, Demeter was always distinguished from other great goddesses, such as Gaia, who represented the entire created order. Gaia was mistress of what today we would call the whole earth. She was an archaic deity, whose genealogy may run all the way back to the Late Stone Age. Because of her very primitive origins, and extremely vague and generalized role in Greek religion, the actual worship of Gaia quickly died out during the period of recorded history. In contrast, Demeter emerged as a personage commanding great loyalty and adoration.

More specifically, Demeter (the suffix "-meter" can be translated as "mother") was known as the divine power by which grain sprouts from the dead kernels. She was the source of all the earth's fruits, and was closely identified with the invention and maintenance of agriculture.

But the significance of Demeter in the ancient Mediterranean world cannot be separated from the paired worship of her daughter Persephone, the corn maiden. Some researchers, in fact, have suggested that Demeter and Persephone must be viewed as two commensurate aspects of the same goddess. But the historical evidence indicates that the rites of worship surrounding the figure of the maiden gradually came to dominate over the older cult of the mother—whatever that may have been.

The ceremonies venerating Demeter and Persephone took place annually at a site selected for its deep underground chasms about twenty miles west of Athens. The place, then as well as now, was known as Eleusis. These ceremonies formed the gist of what have come to be termed the Eleusian mysteries.

The Eleusian mysteries performed the same very important, civic, high religious function for Athens during the five centuries before Christ as the Catholic Mass during the late Middle Ages and the Renaissance. The difference, however, is that Mass was public, whereas the mysteries were secret, even though a huge portion of the population took part in them. For an initiate of the mysteries to divulge what went on was strictly forbidden. And it was only with the coming of the Christian era, when the prestige of the mysteries had eroded and enforcement of such a rigorous code of silence diminished, that some scattered reports or hints of information about the actual ceremonies began to surface.[1]

There are, of course, no eyewitness accounts from which to draw extensive conclusions, and any contemporary theological reflection about Eleusis must remain speculative. On the other hand, it is recorded that most of the great leaders, philosophers, and citizens of Athens were inducted at some time into the mysteries. Moreover, certain key passages from the "middle dialogues" of Plato, to whom the philosopher Alfred North Whitehead dubbed the entire Western intellectual tradition a footnote, were configured by the experiences at Eleusis.[2]

The word "Eleusis" means "the place of happy arrival" and is connected at both the mythical and linguistic levels with a belief in the passage of departed souls to the underworld. The Greek expression "Elysian," which came to refer to that place where those who had lived just and pure lives repaired for eternity—a forerunner of the Christian picture of heaven—is derived from the same term.

The Eleusian mysteries were divided into two dramatic segments coinciding with harvest and seedtime. The lesser mysteries were staged in the spring and the great mysteries, in which the ultimate revelation, *epopteia*, was given, during the autumn. The Greek historian Herodotus claimed the festival at Eleusis had been first practiced by the aboriginal inhabitants of the Greek peninsula, who learned it from the Egyptians.

Archaeologists have deduced that the mysteries were founded on an ancient rite called the *Thesmophoria*, a "laying down of the law."

The law was not that of a father-god but of Demeter and involved the now forgotten statutes of a matriarchal society based on the cultivation of the soil. In addition, pigs were laid down in the deep clefts in the earth at Eleusis and left to die as a sacrificial act designed to invigorate the subterranean forces of fertility and to ensure the growth of crops.

In a later tradition the beliefs associated with the pig sacrifice was transformed symbolically into the story of Persephone, the *korē*, "maiden," abducted by Ploutos, lord of the underworld, and carried down into the bowels of the earth, where she became his bride.

According to the myth, Persephone's "mother," Demeter, went searching for her daughter, whom she finally found in the depths of Hades. Demeter wound up making an agreement with Ploutos that allowed the maiden to return from the nether darkness to the realm of light for half the year. The reunion of mother and daughter was supposedly one of the dramatic highlights of the Eleusian celebration.

A number of psychologists have read into this myth the ideal of a unity behind the different dimensions of the divine, or archetypal, feminine. Kore is youth and sexual beauty. Demeter is age and matronly wisdom. The coming together of the two polarities in this particular concept of the goddess underscores the way in which the ultimate meaning of womanhood resides in neither procreation nor virginity, neither maturity nor innocence, but in their synthesis. The Eleusian mysteries, therefore, replicated at their core what may be regarded as women's mysteries. Such a view, however, ignores the complexity and the social purpose of the shrine and activities at Eleusis.

First, Eleusis was not a cult for women only, or even for them primarily. It was attended and in large measure presided over by men. Contemporary feminists, responding to the present-day psychological needs of women to forge an identity for themselves apart from patriarchal definitions and structures, have tended to look upon pre-Christian goddess religion as an antique form of gender therapy.

But the weight of historical data supports an interpretation of Eleusis as a mythic and ritualized centering of Greek piety on the *feminine side of godhood in its totality*. Furthermore, while Eleusis gave priority to the saga of the two goddesses, it did not exclude the masculine principle of divinity. One version of what occurred in the underground ritual chambers points to a sacred marriage involving sexual intercourse between priest and priestess, leading to the birth of a "holy" male child, who could have been the Greek god Dionysus.

Second, and most important, however, the Eleusian mysteries were very highly regarded because they afforded the participants the experience, and confirmation, of *personal immortality*. The mystical "sight" of the maiden enjoyed by the initiate was tantamount to his or her acquisition of what Christianity would call eternal life. Indeed, if such popular and widespread Mediterranean mystery cults as those of Demeter and Persephone, or Isis and Osiris, had not flourished up through the lifetime of Jesus, the mass appeal and rapid spread of the fledgling Christian religion would have been impossible.

The root metaphors of the Eleusian faith—the dying of the ear of wheat, the disappearance of the kernels in the dark earth, their resurrection in springtime, and the granting of a deathless existence to whoever understands this mystery—are also the sum and substance of Christianity. For example, Jesus' own disclosure of the secret of "life eternal" has strong resonances with the Eleusian religion:

> I tell you, a grain of wheat remains a solitary grain unless it falls into the ground and dies; but if it dies, it bears a rich harvest. The man who loves himself is lost, but he who hates himself in this world will be kept safe for eternal life. (John 12:24–25)

Or consider Paul's exhortation to the Corinthians:

> But, you may ask, how are the dead raised? In what kind of body? How foolish! The seed you sow does not come to life unless it has first died; and what you sow is not the body that shall be, but a naked grain, perhaps of wheat, or of some other kind; and God clothes it with the body of his choice, each

seed with its own particular body. . . . What is sown in the earth as a perishable thing is raised imperishable. (1 Cor. 15:35–39, 42)

Until religious scholars of the current generation began unraveling the pale threads of connection between old forms of goddess worship and key motifs found in the Bible, these kinds of passages were taken primarily as agricultural metaphors employed by male evangelists to persuade a pastoral population. But the notion that allusions within scripture to the divine feminine are wholly rhetorical is rapidly giving way to a more profuse appreciation of the way in which early Christian preaching and teaching not only mirrored the already gendered religious thinking of its milieu, but also was shaped by that type of thinking.

The contemporary view that both Judaism and Christianity were rigidly patriarchal systems of belief and practice that somehow suppressed, or muscled out, a host of native religions just does not stand up to the historical evidence. While it cannot be denied that both Judaism and Christianity have always been patriarchal with respect to their images of God and their social attitudes toward women, it is true as well that the growth and spread of patriarchy during the approximately five millennia preceding and following the birth of Christ has been a social process independent of those belief systems.

Progressively careful scrutiny of the myths of other religious groups during the protracted period when the biblical canon developed has led to a new understanding of how these monotheistic, male-dominated outlooks absorbed, as much as displaced, their more feminine counterparts.

The inference one may make from certain language in the New Testament that many of the key attributes of Mediterranean goddesses, such as the Greek Demeter and the Egyptian Queen of Heaven, Isis, were transferred during the first few centuries of the Christian era to the exalted Jesus has now been fairly well established. When those feminine traits began to fade from orthodox theology in the late Roman Empire, particularly when Catholicism came under heavy Germanic influence after the barbarian invasions, the imbalance was redressed through the cult of the Virgin Mary.

In point of fact, Christianity as a persecuted sect could not have spread so quickly on its own during the early centuries without the help of imperial decrees if it did not already carry many of the implicit messages and attitudes of the popular religions of the ancient world. These popular religions were, as it turned out, largely salvation cults or mystery cults centered on goddess figures or their sons and consorts.

The Golden Ass

The most dramatic account of the experience of redemption by the goddess is found in *The Golden Ass* by the North African writer Apuleius, who lived during the middle decades of the second century of the Roman era. *The Golden Ass* is a kind of ancient comic romance novel that recites the adventures of the author within the religious underworld of Roman imperial society. The book vividly describes the numerous and flourishing religious cults of the time.

The story tells of Apuleius's bewitchment at the hands of a witch, or sorceress, who turned him into a donkey, and his eventual salvation by the great Egyptian goddess Isis. The tale of Apuleius's dramatic vision of and conversion to the goddess exhibits the same ancient psychology that ensured the propagation and acceptance of the doctrine of a new "savior"—Jesus Christ.

Apuleius first prays to Isis, who he says holds sway over all of "providence" and "all bodies on the earth." The prayer even includes a reference to Demeter and Persephone.

> I lifted my tear-wet face in supplication to the irresistible Goddess: "Queen of Heaven, whether you are fostering Ceres the motherly nurse of all growth, who (gladdened at the discovery of your lost daughter), abolished the brutish nutriment of the primitive acorn and pointed the way to gentler food (as is yet shown in the tilling of the fields of Eleusis); or whether you are celestial Venus who in the first moment of Creation mingled the opposing sexes in the generation of mutual desires, and who (after sowing in humanity the seeds of indestructible continuing life) are now worshipped in the wave-washed shrine of Paphos. . . . Support my broken life, and give me rest and peace after the tribulations of my lot. Let there be an end to the toils that weary me, and an end to the snares that beset me. . . . Restore me to Lucius, my lost self."[3]

In response to Lucius's petition, the goddess appears and declares:

> Behold, Lucius . . . moved by your prayer I come to you—I, the natural mother of all life, the mistress of the elements, the first child of time, the supreme divinity, the queen of those in hell, the first among those in heaven, the uniform manifestation of all the gods and goddesses. . . . I, whose single godhead is venerated all over the earth under manifold forms, varying rites, and changing names. . . . Behold, I am come to you in your calamity. I am come with solace and aid. Away then with tears. . . . Eternal religion has dedicated to me the day which will be born from the womb of this present darkness."[4]

The supernatural power of the savior mother, whose attributions compare favorably to early liturgical language about Jesus, served as the context in which the doctrines of the early church became appealing to the Gentiles. What Isis worship was to the Africans, the Eleusian religion was to Greeks on the northern shores of the Mediterranean.

Indeed, there is evidence of direct Egyptian influence on the Eleusian mythology around the sixth century.[5] On the other hand, as the testimony of Apuleius suggests, the different names for the great goddess in different parts of the known world were viewed as arbitrary.

Like Christianity, these goddess religions were universalistic faiths inasmuch as they drew, and welcomed, adherents of all nationalities, social classes, and previous religious beliefs. Like Christianity, they stressed a personal and passionate relationship with a redeemer who possessed gentle, cosmic qualities. Like Christianity, they sought to weld the entirety of humankind into a new "body" of believers.

In one respect *The Golden Ass* can be read in the same manner as the New Testament books of Luke and Acts—as a continuous, and detailed, account of the mysterious workings of the savior deity amid the chaotic and disintegrating culture of the day. The connections between Isis worship and the traditions of Judaism and Christianity during the first two centuries were fairly strong.

The major intellectual center of the imperial age was Alexandria in Egypt, where much of the basic theological architecture of those two faiths was hammered out. Today the Alexandrian character of so much early Christian theology is finally beginning to be appreciated. If devotion to the North African Queen of Heaven was as extensive in the Nile delta as the veneration of Mary in medieval France, then it is quite reasonable to assume, contrary to certain dogmatic prejudices, that the mythic shadow of Isis hangs over Alexandrian Judaism and Christianity.

The Eleusian Mysteries and the Book of Ruth

However, there is another strange and interesting tie-in between the Eleusian mysteries themselves and the tradition surrounding Jesus that has been scarcely noted by biblical interpreters. These alliances have been carefully analyzed by G.R.H. Wright in a relatively recent article published in Germany.[6] According to Wright, the legend of Demeter and Persephone is echoed strongly, and not merely accidentally, in the book of Ruth.

The book of Ruth tells about a Jewish woman, Naomi, from the town of Bethlehem in Judah, who while in flight from a famine journeys with her husband and two sons to the heathen Canaanite kingdom of Moab. In Moab, Naomi's husband dies, and the two sons marry Moabite women, Orpah and Ruth.

Eventually the two sons die, and Naomi decides to go back to Bethlehem to live out the remainder of her life with her kinsmen, who are now prospering. She bids her two daughters-in-law to stay in Moab with their families, but Ruth refuses to leave Naomi's side, thus demonstrating her loyalty to the Jewish side of the family. Once Naomi and Ruth are back in Judah, an issue of who shall inherit some land owned by the family arises.

In a complex series of events a man named Boaz, one of Naomi's male kinsmen, rescues the family's patrimony by marrying Ruth. Boaz, it is later pointed out, was the great-grandfather of King David and, as the opening genealogy in the Gospel of Matthew notes, the ancestor of Jesus.

Scholars have pondered the meaning and importance of the book of Ruth, which may have been composed only a few centuries before Christianity. But one likely rendition is that the tale of Ruth couples the lineage of the Messiah to foreign women from cultures steeped in heathen fertility practices and beliefs.

The fear that intermarriage might snuff out the pure seed of Abraham was rife after the destruction of the Temple at Jerusalem and the deportation of the Jews to Babylon during the sixth century B.C.E. The book of Ruth may have been written not merely to allay such anxieties but to emphasize how God's chosen and anointed did not need to be of flawless stock.

Certainly such revisionist perspectives on the messianic bloodline were crucial to the claims of the early Christians about the legitimacy of Jesus. At the same time, as Wright suggests, the story may also reflect hidden cultural cross-stitchings between the ceremonies of Eleusis, which constituted the "archetypal internationalised mystery religion for the Hellenic world," and some more esoteric threads within mainline Judaism itself. In fact, the similarities between the account of Ruth and Naomi and the myth of Persephone and Demeter are more than intriguing.

For example, both the drama of Eleusis and the tale of Ruth center on the close and unbroken relationship between an older and a younger woman. Both Eleusis and Bethlehem, from which Naomi's family came, were grain-growing centers and may at different times have been fertility cult centers as well. Even though barley was grown in Palestine and wheat in Greece, the religious associations were the same in both places.[7]

In Cretan versions of the mother and maid myth, Persephone gave birth to a divine child called either Ploutos or Dionysus. The book of Ruth is about a sexual liaison that makes possible the eventual birth of the divine king. Both the Eleusian mystery and the Palestinian "folktale" focus on the immortal bond between two women as the key to future life and the secrets of generation.

Wright suggests that the messianic ideas of early Christianity, which differed significantly from the patriarchal themes of Jewish orthodoxy, may have been inspired by a common Mediterranean—and we may add matriarchal—form of religious culture which, though essentially nonliterate, heavily influenced the popular imagination of both the Greeks and the church. Wright concludes with special attention to what he calls the "later historical developments of the Bethlehem cult." He notes:

> The ultimate version of the cult has become truly universal, the avowed aim of all mystery religions. The virgin *mater dolorosa* was required to return to Bethlehem, the house of bread, to give birth to the divine child who was

laid in a manger exactly as Dionysos Liknites was laid on the winnowing fan at Eleusis to ensure that those who hungered should be filled—with bread.[8]

Hidden behind the Christian nativity legends is a religious conflict that was as old as the contest between patriarchy and matriarchy running back thousands of years.

Orthodox Judaism, then and later, sought to ground the hope for universal salvation in the coming of a male messiah, an exemplar of righteousness, who would exert a commanding, regal, and strong moral authority in the world. The Messiah would be part of the people's patrimony and of the male lineage of David. However, in the matriarchal myth, salvation lay in the conservation of the bond between feminine age and youth, in the protection of maidenhood for the sake of the earth's fecundity, and in the alliance between mature wisdom and sexual precocity.

It is interesting that both the Eleusian and Christian story lines revolve around immaculate conceptions, or the procreation of a divine male figure without a fertilizing father. The myth of immaculate conception was quite common in matriarchal religion and reflected the feeling of magical power ascribed to the life-giving body of the mother.

It is even more interesting, on the other hand, that in the Nativity narrative at the opening of the Gospel of Matthew, which tells "the story of the birth of the Messiah," the father of Jesus finds that his fiancée, Mary, is pregnant, though not by him, and "being a man of principle, and at the same time wanting to save her from exposure, Joseph desired to have the marriage contract set aside quietly" (Matt. 1:18–19). Joseph only relents when an angel appears to him in a dream and tells him that "it is by the Holy Spirit that she has conceived this child" (Matt. 1:20).

Now Joseph, according to Matthew's genealogy, was a direct descendant of both David and of the union of Ruth and Boaz. The prospect of his future wife giving birth to a child who was not "his own" threatened the very Jewish principle of messianic redemption through the male line.

At the same time, it is clear that the early Christian solution to this dilemma served to import and sanctify the values of the Mediterranean worship of the divine feminine. The somewhat paradoxical figure of the man Jesus recorded in the Gospels—the gentle, humble, politically inconsequential, itinerant teacher who in the same vein assumed the mantle of the mighty, masculine scion of David—may point to the confluence of these two religious strains.

Furthermore, Jesus' passion on the cross, not to mention the redemptive significance it bore in the minds of the people of his time, fit the archetypal Mediterranean agricultural myth of the dying and rising god, as religious historians have long known. In the distinctively Christian story, therefore, we have not just the transformation of the Semitic warrior deity into the God of love; we also discern a powerful and unprecedented *amalgamation of matriarchal and patriarchal religious meanings* that had been at loggerheads with each other ever since the Stone Age, perhaps even through the whole of prehistory.

It must be granted that this amalgamation was only achieved through the merger of the matriarchal elements with the patriarchal ideal of the triumphant warrior God, the *Christus Victor,* who fights the final battle with evil in the book of Revelation.

In addition, this consolidation was inevitable because of the bald historical fact that has been the stumbling block for any efforts of conservative feminists to retain the elements of traditional Christianity—Jesus was male!

But it also underscores that what we have called the hermeneutical dilemma of contemporary Christian faith, which appears to stand in the way of a true liberation of the power and spirit of women, is not as refractory as it may look at eye level. While Jesus was in fact a man, he played the part of the antitype to the male messiah who would secure the future of patriarchy.

In present-day jargon, Jesus deconstructed the myth of patriarchy by the way he shaped through his life and actions the messianic script. Under the cover of the "Son of David," he performed in the capacity of Dionysus, son of Persephone. And it was in the latter guise that his legacy was able to sweep across the Mediterranean with awesome speed and force and to transmute the exclusivistic Judaic ideal of the "seed of Abraham" into the universalistic expectation of salvation for all those who, as Paul put it, "died in Christ" and were reborn, like the kernels of corn, through him.

Sophia and Alexandrian Judaism

Yet the biography of the historical Jesus could not have been so decisive had it not been for the presence in Roman Palestine of another powerful goddess who bore the Greek name Sophia.

The mythic origins of Sophia are quite obscure and have been the subject of wide-ranging academic debate. The most likely explanation is that Sophia, or Wisdom, was the Greek name given to a divine figure whose cult was rooted in the religious soil of Egypt. The figure indeed may originally have been Isis herself,[9] although she was transformed under the influence of Alexandrian Judaism into a hybrid personality that combined the traditions surrounding the Israelite concept of the divine presence of Shekinah and the idea of cosmic wisdom, or *Hokhma.*

While the mythic notion of divine wisdom is present throughout the Old Testament, it is only in the few centuries preceding the rise of Christianity that it appears to have become an actual focus of worship.

The literary context for what may be called the Gospel of Sophia is situated primarily in the Wisdom of Solomon, a so-called intertestamental book of the Bible that was written in Greek during the first century of the Christian era.

The Wisdom of Solomon is part of the Apocrypha, a body of writings that was not accepted into the Jewish canon because it was authored in Greek rather than Hebrew and, hence, was not officially part of the English Bible, although it was included in the Roman Catholic scripture. The Wisdom of Solomon clearly displays the synthesis of Greek and Hebrew thought that served as the backdrop for so much of New Testament writing and reflection.

The Wisdom of Solomon is addressed to the "rulers of the earth" and takes the form of a prophetic declamation against political arrogance and social injustice. But other passages strongly suggest, as a footnote in the *New English Bible* makes clear, that the audience is the Jewish settlement in Alexandria.[10]

Like much of New Testament theology itself, the Wisdom of Solomon is an attempt to reinterpret the Old Testament history of God's mysterious dealings with "his" chosen people in the light of contemporary experience and circumstances. Just as various works of the New Testament—for example, Paul's letter to the Romans and the book of Hebrews—consist in radical new forms of salvation history which revolve around the life and death of Jesus the Christ, so the Wisdom of Solomon challenges Jewish readers to consider afresh what has occurred in the past as the constant ministration, and intervention, of the divine Sophia.

"Wisdom is a spirit devoted to man's good" (Wisd. Sol. 1:6), the anonymous author of the book writes, and goes on to identify Sophia with the "spirit of the LORD" or Holy Spirit, an association that also occurs in Colossians 1:17 and in Hebrews 1:3. Wisdom is the teacher of humanity (Wisd. Sol. 6:17). "She is quick to make herself known to those who desire knowledge of her" (Wisd. Sol. 6:13).

"For in wisdom there is a spirit intelligent and holy, unique in its kind yet made up of many parts, subtle, free-moving, lucid, spotless, clear, invulnerable, loving what is good, eager, unhindered, beneficent, kindly towards men, steadfast, unerring, untouched by care, all-powerful, all-surveying, and permeating all intelligent, pure, and delicate spirits" (Wisd. Sol. 7:22–24).

Wisdom mirrors the very creative power of God; "she pervades and permeates all things because she is so pure," an "effulgence from the glory of the Almighty" (Wisd. Sol. 7:24–25). "She is but one, yet can do everything; herself unchanging, she makes all things new; age after age she enters into holy souls, and makes them God's friends and prophets" (Wisd. Sol. 7:26–27).

Older types of biblical exegesis commonly played down the gender-specific language of this dramatic section of scripture, characterizing it as a feminine personification of an abstract attribute of the Hebrew

Deity. But more recent research, aided by data from the study of ancient Near Eastern religion *in toto,* supports the view that the praises of Sophia are much more concrete than has been hitherto presupposed.

Whether Sophia was actually worshiped by the writer of the Wisdom of Solomon remains in dispute. But it is apparent from the text itself that she is more than a metaphor or literary affectation. A minimal consensus nowadays holds that the intertestamental Sophia is an adaptation of the traditional Jewish idea of the Shekinah, or divine presence, which was taken as a feminine in nature.

Yet there are other indications such a presence took on a personality of her own. For example, the author, who purports to be Solomon himself, known for his countless wives and lovers, tells of encountering her after passionate prayer and supplication.

Whether the historic Solomon actually venerated this divine personality, which is itself not out of the question, cannot really be ascertained. However, the key to understanding the religious importance of Sophia can be located in Wisdom of Solomon 8, where the author says that "in kinship with wisdom lies immortality" (Wisd. Sol. 8:17).

The appeal of the different goddess cults, including the Isis, throughout imperial times, was their promise to the devotee of immortal existence, as the evidence from Eleusis and the tale of Apuleius dramatically shows. In the case of the Jews in Egypt the problem was that of the immortality of their chosen race, threatened not only by the dire political events in Palestine, but by growing unbelief and the dangers of assimilation by a hostile Gentile world, which have persisted down into the modern world.

Alexandrian Jewry, unlike its counterparts in Judea, did not regard the destiny of the people in terms of the survival of the Palestinian state and the centrality of the Temple at Jerusalem. Significantly, the Wisdom of Solomon concentrates on the lessons of the exodus and the period preceding the rise of the Davidic monarchy, while the political idea of Messiahship first arose.

In the Wisdom of Solomon, the overall salvation of the Jewish people is couched in terms of preserving a direct relationship between God and the people, especially the lowly and the oppressed.

It was Sophia, acting as the image of the invisible God, who "rescued a godfearing people, a blameless race, from a nation of oppressors; she inspired a servant of the LORD, and with his signs and wonders he defied formidable kings" (Wisd. Sol. 10:15–16). The last citation is far more radical than it seems on the surface, because it implies that the God of Moses, who in Exodus identifies himself also as the "God of Abraham, Isaac, and Jacob," is actually Sophia.

In other words, the Jewish-Christian God himself can equally be called she. In the Wisdom of Solomon Sophia clearly performs the role of *soter,* "saviour," and possesses many of the attributes that the New Testament writers later ascribed to Jesus.

In the last decade or so biblical scholarship has uncovered some startling evidence that Jesus himself, or at least the post-Easter traditions surrounding Jesus, can be linked with this Sophia tradition. According to Richard Horsley, Sophia is the "vortex" of the whole pattern of early Christian religious thinking.[11] She is the "very content" of salvation.

As the historical theologian Elisabeth Schüssler Fiorenza points out, "Sophia theology" not only sought to integrate goddess piety into the Jewish religion, it also became the basis for the proclamation of the Christian community "that all distinctions of a religion, race, class, nationality, and gender are insignificant."[12]

Finally, we have the observation of the noted biblical scholar James M. Robinson that there was a long-standing tenet among Jews that Sophia was the source and inspiration of all true prophets. This idea, manifest in the Wisdom of Solomon, culminates in sayings from the Gospel of Luke, where Jesus, along with John the Baptist, is portrayed as one of her "children."[13]

Certain themes in early Gnostic Christianity, which was later condemned as heterodox, stress that Sophia was actually Jesus' brother in the heavenly realm. Jesus came to rescue her from the powers of darkness.[14]

In the New Testament itself, nonetheless, Jesus himself is assimilated in key passages to Sophia.[15] And in the so-called hymns to Christ found in different books of the New Testament the comparison is pronounced. According to Schüssler Fiorenza, these hymns were not new, but belonged to what she calls a "reflective mythology" of ancient civilization that was "borrowed primarily from the [Egyptian] myth of Isis-Osiris,"[16] which was first Judaized as the story of Sophia.

Mythically, if not in fact, Jesus becomes Sophia, but he also reflects the values and the devotion of the Queen of Heaven. As another scholar has put it, the earliest Christian theology was tantamount to "study of the wisdom goddess."[17] There is evidence that about the time of Jesus there actually was a sect of Judaism that worshiped Sophia, even though its possible connections with early Christianity are rather vague.

This sect was known as the Therapeutae and was comprised of both celibate men and women living together in the same desert community. Because veneration of Sophia was fairly common within the Jewish tradition at the time, the Therapeutae were not eccentric outsiders or cultists but mainstream believers who, like the Essenes that left us the Dead Sea Scrolls at Qumran, had distanced themselves from what they perceived as the corrupt establishment in Jerusalem and created their own holy order in the wilderness.

The faithful of the community, who probably relied on the Wisdom of Solomon as one of their key texts, practiced what was called the *synousia*, "spiritual marriage," with Sophia. It should be pointed out that certain Christian nuns in the Middle Ages also practiced a spiritual marriage with their "bridegroom" Jesus.

The spiritual marriage of the Therapeutae hinged on the conviction that the soul can be united deeply and intimately, as in actual sexual intercourse, with Sophia, or Lady Wisdom. Only through such an act of "knowledge" can the sage truly experience what, or who, God is. Such a theological perspective could be found in some guise throughout Alexandrian Judaism, and it fomented the context for what Philo called the "wisdom mystery," the sowing of the "seed of Sophia" in the sacred race of Abraham.[18]

Sophia and Early Christianity

The idea of such a "mystery" apparently arose within the religion of Isis and was adapted by Alexandrian Judaism.[19] Through a "divine marriage" Jews would be initiated into the secret and would possess the immortality granted by Isis/Sophia. They too would achieve as part of their very human substance the lineage and "matrimony" of Sophia.

God's promise to Israel would be secured, as Paul would later phrase the matter, not "according to the flesh," but through the Spirit. And as recent research has begun to show quite persuasively, the tradition of the genealogy of the Spirit in late Judaism and early Christianity is closely connected with the heretofore covert religion of Sophia.

In the language of Philo himself, "God is the Father of all things, and the Husband of Sophia, dropping the seed of happiness for the race of mortals into good and virgin soil."[20] In Christian orthodoxy the Holy Spirit is the active power of God that works throughout time to bring the drama of the creation to its intended end.

In the wisdom literature the same function is assigned to Sophia. Furthermore, the dove, which is the conventional Christian symbol of the Holy Spirit, is also associated with Sophia and other goddess figures of ancient civilization.

This imagery persisted for centuries down into the European Middle Ages. An illuminated manuscript from the Eynsham Abbey in Oxfordshire, England, that dates to the twelfth century depicts Sophia with a child in her lap seated on a lion throne. In her right hand she holds a lily, and atop the lily sits a dove.

According to the manuscript, Sophia is the "root of all things." Through the "spiritual marriage" of the soul to Sophia eternal life and happiness is seen as possible. It is known, of course, that Sophia religion had a strong influence on Gnostic Christianity. Various Gnostic documents, including the complex tome known as the *Pistis Sophia,* speak in different ways of a mysterious divine figure called Wisdom who descends to earth and becomes a kind of savior figure in her own right.

The Gnostic Sophia, of course, is significantly different from the personage who appears in the Wisdom of Solomon.[21] And much of the hidden agenda behind the theological arguments found in Paul over the meanings of such terms as "spirit" and "wisdom" may have to do with this distinction.

For instance, in Paul's first letter to the Corinthians there is the well-known controversy over what it means to be "spirit-filled." It is apparent that Paul is responding to a community within whom are Gnostic Christians who have come to believe that what one does "in the body" is immaterial because they have attained a spiritual marriage with Sophia.[22]

To the Corinthians Paul insists that "wisdom" and "spiritual truth" are not private possessions of the illuminated, but attributes of corporate life in the "body of Christ." Paul grounds this corporate theology, in opposition to Gnostic pride and exclusivism, in a new doctrine of wisdom that he identifies with the crucified Jesus.

This "divine wisdom" he contrasts with the "wisdom of the world." He calls Christ "our wisdom," literally "our Sophia" (1 Cor. 1:30). The cross is "God's hidden wisdom, his secret purpose framed from the very beginning to bring us to our full glory" (1 Cor. 2:7–8). In subsequent passages the uncovering of this wisdom is "revealed to us through the Spirit."

In other words, Paul himself combines the essential notion of God's death on the cross with the Sophia tradition. If the theme, resonant in the opening verses of the Gospel of John, that through Jesus the "Word became flesh" can be traced directly to the thought of Philo of Alexandria, as most scholars agree, then it is also evidence of the origins of the fundamental Christian doctrine of incarnation in Sophia piety itself.

As it happens, Philo was quite familiar with the community of Therapeutae, who devoted themselves to Sophia, and he may even have studied with them. The Therapeutae may even have been the source of the wisdom hymns in the Pauline tradition.[23] As Baring and Cashford observe in their historical survey of the old goddess religion, "Jesus Christ, as the incarnate 'Word,' son of the heavenly father, assumes the qualities that once belonged to Sophia."[24]

Because the word "wisdom," which takes the neuter gender in English, is used to translate the Greek *Sophia* as it recurs throughout the New Testament, the more primordial association between the incarnational thought of the early church and the Hebraic divine female has been lost.

The outlook shared by many early Christians placed Sophia in close relationship to God himself, as the divine nurturer, as the minister and helpmate of the heavenly father, even as his wife, lover, or mistress—depending on the context. But, even more strikingly, God is willing to share his beloved with all who seek her. Like the "Word" in the Gospel of John, she "dwelt" or "tented" with Israel; she made the people her "inheritance" (Wisd. Sol. 8:3).

The allusion, of course, is to the close, physical relationship enjoyed by a tribal group to a female "camp follower," and the references to Lady Wisdom occurring in Proverbs call to mind the habits of an ancient streetwalker. As Caitlín Matthews observes, "the line between the street-

walking whore looking for trade and the diligent wife seeking her husband is a fine one" in the imagery of Sophia from the Bible.[25]

To begin with, married women in the ancient world generally did not
"call aloud in the streets," as Sophia does. Furthermore, they did not
hang out with groups of men. The one who did, and who ironically typ-
ifies the human role of Sophia, was Mary Magdalene, a prostitute. While
this kind of figurative diction does not suggest that early Christianity either encouraged or condoned loose-living women, it underscores the
radical change in social thinking and gender awareness that went along
with the emergence of Christianity.

Under patriarchy the male is fearful and remote, while his wives and
daughters are both bound tightly in a family structure and protected as
part of a code of honor. That ethic was not only common in traditional
Judaism, it also defined the nature of God and his teaching, or Torah.

In the Sophia religion and in early Christianity, however, God becomes freely available as a loving and intimate companion, or at least
his "wife" is so available. Rigid structures of propriety, ownership, and
authority that distance both the divine and human, and human beings
from each other, are broken down. Sophia as teacher is the friend of all,
and she does not shrink from sharing her innermost self with all those
who seek her, even if it is the intimacy of divine knowledge rather than
the fleeting sort of carnal knowledge purveyed by a woman of the
streets.

Sophia's open-armed love and offerings of intimacy are so great that
she even risks scorn and abuse. The reception accorded to Jesus parallels what the wisdom tradition describes as the attitude of the ignorant
toward Sophia.

In short, the biblical Sophia is an intimate partner with the male sex
and, even from a heavenly standpoint, is equal in stature to him, while
she acts independently. Ironically, it was later Gnostic theory that turned
Sophia into a rival divinity to the Jewish male figure of God while down-
playing the importance and sanctity of the body.

It was the Gnostic myth that transformed Sophia into an unap-
proachable virgin goddess who appears more as holy mother than as sensual wife or lover. Such a myth became the basis for the medieval por-
trait of the Virgin Mary and for the legends of chaste knights questing
after spiritual perfection in the form of the Holy Grail. These legends
usually entail the fleeting ministries of a mysterious and inaccessible
woman, such as Kundry in the Parsifal tale made into a famous opera by
Richard Wagner.

The woman corresponds to the Gnostic Sophia. She guards the secrets of eternal life, and she demands of the male "knight" in search of
her an oath of abstinence and purity. While feminist writers have
frequently extolled the Gnostic goddess as an alternative to the male
Jewish-Christian God for women to reverence, the unpleasant historical
truth is that such systems of belief have usually been violent and cruel,

even to women. The use of the Parsifal story by the Nazis is a case in point.

Jesus and Sophia

The Sophia of popular Judaism, nevertheless, has a different cachet. Like Isis, Sophia was the divine female who cared for *all* her children, and took an exceptional interest in the abandoned and downtrodden. The social and moral prescriptions of the teacher Jesus—himself the "child" of the Great Teacher Sophia—echo this approach. And we must seriously examine the degree to which the Jesus of the Gospels, and not just of the wisdom liturgies found in the Pauline letters, actually took on the garb and role of Sophia herself.

The major issue facing New Testament scholarship has always been Jesus' own understanding of himself. Christian tradition has always emphasized his appropriation of the messianic title Son of David, or Son of God, which his antagonists mocked during his crucifixion by making him wear the crown of thorns and the inscription "King of the Jews."

Still, the majority of scholars concur that during his career at least Jesus preferred the appellation "Son of Man"—a curious and enigmatic title that can only be found in the so-called apocalyptic writings of the Old Testament and Apocrypha, such as the books of Daniel and Ezekiel.

Over a generation ago the Old Testament scholar James Muilenburg identified Jesus' self-designation "Son of Man" as more than an honorific epithet.[26] The idea of the Son of Man is integrally bound up with the Sophia legacy, according to Muilenburg.

Jesus, therefore, calls himself the "son" of the divine figure Anthropos, "Humanity," who in the Gnostic myth is the "immortal Adam," an identification to which Paul also alludes in different passages. But in other versions of the same myth, as well as in Philo and Job, Anthropos is also called "Sophia," who is a redeemer figure in her own right.[27] *Hence, Jesus as Son of Man is also "Son of Sophia."* For "the time of salvation is the time of wisdom: the Son of Man is the bearer of [Sophia]."[28]

The Jewish assimilation of the divine redeemer figure to Sophia explains why, according to a group of feminist biblical interpreters, the writer of John gives Sophia the new name of God's "Word," then proceeds to identify her with Jesus. They note that John 1:14, which says that the Word "became flesh" and "come to dwell" among humanity, echoes word for word what Sophia says she is doing in Ecclesiasticus 24:8: "Then the Creator of the universe laid a command upon me. . . . Make your home in Jacob; find your heritage in Israel.' "

They stress that "this identification of Jesus Creator Incarnate with Sophia Creator Incarnate in John is nearly as dramatic as Paul's direct statement that Jesus is our Sophia."[29] Moreover, Sophia herself was understood in her day as "a co-creator with the Hebrew God," as a "messenger from God, and she is God's lover."[30]

What is distinctive about the Gospel of John is the way in which Jesus constantly and self-assuredly proclaims his intimacy with the Father. Such proclamations, however, are characteristic of what Sophia says about herself. If Jesus is the only way to "reach" the Father, as John asserts repeatedly, the connotation is toward Sophia, who plays the same function in the wisdom literature.

When Jesus declares in John 10:37–38 that he is doing his father's work, it is another reverberation of Sophia theology found in the Judaism of the period. Both Jesus and Sophia were dispatched by God on an important, cosmic mission. The implication is that Jesus, the Hebrew God, and Sophia are all part of the same intimate family circle.

It is in this connection that the strange and, to some, disturbing attitude of John toward whom he simply calls the "Jews" may thus become intelligible. If Jesus and his followers are the seed of Sophia, they are of a different race in the spiritual sense, one that can trace its ancestry not through the minions of patriarchy, but through holy women.

In Matthew's genealogy, Jesus' descent is explicitly traced through a number of harlots, including Tamar and Rahab. And Sophia, like other independent goddesses, was also known to raise people from the dead. Jesus' statements in John that he is the "truth" and the "life," not to mention his ability to perform miracles, has strong affinities with the Gnostic characterization of Sophia.[31]

Finally, Jesus' description of himself as the "living water" (John 4:11) and as the "bread of life" (John 6:35) resounds with the theme found in Sirach of "[Sophia] as nourisher."[32] The image of the "bread of life," in addition, recalls the harvest cult at Bethlehem, where David lived and Jesus was born, and which would have invoked memories of the great Demeterian religious complex of the Mediterranean basin with its unique gift of eternal life for votaries.

A German scholar by the name of Felix Christ has shown that numerous passages from the Synoptic Gospels—Matthew, Mark, and Luke—cannot be understood except as "sayings of Sophia" through the mouth of Jesus. For example, when Jesus says in Matthew 11:30 that "my yoke is good to bear, my load is light," the reference is to what the writer of Ecclesiasticus tells of Sophia: "Give your shoulder to her yoke. . . . For in the end you will find rest in her" (Ecclus. 51:26).[33]

It is clear in much of the Synoptic Gospels that Jesus' sense of an imminent end and judgment of the world was strongly configured by the Sophia tradition. Jesus saw himself as the final envoy of Sophia who had sent prophets and messengers to her people, only to have them murdered and scorned.

The evidence for this Sophian background to Jesus' ministry, of course, is Luke 7:31–35, mentioned earlier. Jesus says:

> How can I describe the people of this generation? What are they like? They are like children sitting in the market-place and shouting at each other, "We piped for you and you would dance." "We wept and wailed, and you would not mourn." For John the Baptist came neither eating bread nor drinking wine, and you say, "He is possessed." The Son of Man came eating and drinking, and you say, "Look at him! a glutton and a drinker, a friend of tax-gatherers and sinners!" And yet God's [Sophia] is proved right by all who are her children.

These lines have always proven difficult for New Testament exegetes. But they make eminent sense in the light of what we know about Sophia religion. Sophia is the whore, or street preacher, who is constantly admonishing people in the marketplace. Like Jesus, she is accused of riotous and unseemly behavior, a loose woman who dances and gets drunk at the block party.

The people, in turn, are taunting both her and her son Jesus, whose own behavior may seem indecorous and extreme, but is "proven right" with respect to the ideal of fellowship that marks God's coming kingdom. Jesus' reaching out to and consorting with "sinners" was not an idiosyncrasy on his part. It was befitting of the Son of Man, who was Sophia's representative.

Finally, we can begin to comprehend, even more dramatically, Jesus' use of parables and aphoristic sayings. His employment of pithy, fragmented, or gnomic, forms of communication was characteristic of the wisdom tradition and had analogues in Greece and Egypt.

Just as Sophia herself was coy and elusive, so her communications to humanity were ad hoc and elliptical. The so-called sapiential insight she offered was direct and experiential. It had to come in a flash.

Jesus' proclamation of the impending kingdom and attendant judgment took this rhetorical form. But its style was quite familiar to his hearers. It was a new form of what Ronald Piper called "the old wisdom." The old wisdom had now been recast "eschatologically" by the Son of Sophia. "The old wisdom has been newly grounded in alignment with the announcement of the kingdom."[34]

The *synousia*, "spiritual marriage," with Sophia is, and will be, revealed in the final days as the *parousia*, "full presence," of the "Son of Man" with "great power and glory" (Matt. 24:27–31). It will be as abrupt and dramatic as "lightning from the east, flashing as far as the west." It will be what was intended from the very outset of creation, as Sophia intended.

It is entirely possible, although such a view remains speculative at this juncture, that the presence of this only partially concealed Sophia heritage of the New Testament signifies something more than a mere ensemble of cultural influences. *It may be the cipher that decodes the New Testament itself.*

The matchup between the deeds and utterances of Jesus and the self-ascriptions of Sophia can be construed at one level as typical of the relationship between the ancient Mediterranean goddesses and their male sons/lovers, who often behaved in their stead. It would not have been unusual for Mediterranean peasant folk to hear the voice of a goddess in the prophetic verbiage of her male representative, even if they were Jews.

Palestinian Jews had been familiar with goddess cults for over a millennium. Thus the suspicion that the men of the early church deliberately robbed the early Christian community of its feminine worldview, and heritage, is not well founded.

Something else was going on. And the eventual contraction of the son of Sophia into the exclusively male Jesus, head of a male-dominated church, may have had to do more with the controversy over the eschatological character of the man from Galilee and the true meaning of the term "Christ" (Greek = "messiah").

It is apparent from the Gospel accounts that whatever efforts may have been mounted to convince Jews of the day that Jesus was the legitimate "messianic" heir of David were not very effective. The Sanhedrin and the Jerusalem rabble made fun of such a pretension by the way they brutalized him at Calvary.

The Sunday school review of Jesus' messianic credentials has always emphasized the paradoxical and "scandalous" nature of his divine sonship. But could this "scandal" actually have been the result of an existing conflict, which has since been lost to history, within Judaism itself about the character of the Messiah? We do not at present have all the answers. But we can begin to frame a picture in our mind.

Jesus did in fact see himself as the "Son of Man"—a title that would have been meaningful within an obscure but quite real messianic tradition to which various desert sects such as the Therapeutae subscribed and which also awaited the appearance on earth of the "son of Sophia." Could not the attempt, therefore, to place him within the traditional Davidic line of succession be less important than we realize?

Furthermore, could not the association of Jesus as "the Christ" throughout the writings of Paul and the liturgies of the early church with the wisdom literature of the Bible, and by extension the historical figure of Solomon, who did more than any other hero of the faith to paganize the Hebrew patriarchy by intermarrying and adapting foreign goddess cults, be more than an accidental development?

Is it not possible that in some profound fashion the early church, which regarded itself as the eschatological "seed of Sophia" rather than the "seed of David," turned out to be the fruition of a long-fermenting split within Judaism, perhaps even going back to the days of Solomon, over the character of the Messiah and the messianic kingdom? Is that possibly why Jesus referred to himself as the Son of Man or "Son of Sophia"—the messiah of the Wisdom religion rather than the "Son of God," the title of the Davidic king?[35]

Could not the bone of contention have been the degree to which mas-

culine and feminine sides of the engendering Godhead took prece-
dence, and how this dispute was to be played out in the messianic drama
itself?[36] Is it not possible that contemporary Christians do not have to
find novel and strained strategies for doing feminist readings of the New
Testament, because early Christianity itself contained many of the same,
implicit values that women, as well as men, seek to affirm today?

A Revolutionary Movement
within Judaism

One of the most intriguing sections in the Wisdom of Solomon is the
sixth chapter, where the author admonishes the kings of the earth to
"seek" Sophia and to "love" her through the path of learning. "Thus the
desire of wisdom leads to kingly stature. If, therefore, you value your
thrones and your sceptres, you rulers of nations, you must honour wisdom, so that you may reign for ever" (Wisd. Sol. 6:20–21).

Aside from the looser interpolation that Solomon is proposing the
Hebraic version of Plato's philosopher king—an idea with which in the
milieu of Egyptian Hellenism he may quite likely have been ac-
quainted—these passages imply what may be called eschatological kingship. They are not about the protocols of monarchical administration,
but about the ultimate relationship between divine and human rule.

Sophia, like Isis in Egyptian mythology, bestows title and authority on
the king, who allocates justice at her command.[37] Even in the Jewish tradition wisdom is always attributed to the role of the king. She, in fact, de-
termines who shall be king. She requires "righteousness" as the condi-
tion of continued rule.

Solomon says that in the company of wisdom "I shall leave an undy-
ing memory to those who come after me. I shall rule over many peoples,
and nations will become my subjects" (Wisd. Sol. 8:13–14). It is note-
worthy, of course, that in the book of Kings and in the Deuteronomic
theology the linkage between the historical fortunes of the people of Israel and the righteousness of rulers is construed as an extension of the
Mosaic covenant. The Deuteronomist "rates" the kings of Judah and Israel in the measure that "they did what was right in the sight of
[Yahweh]," which usually means whether they had commerce with foreign cults and installed female deities.

Solomon receives very poor marks in the Deuteronomic account. Yet
in the Wisdom of Solomon he is the mouthpiece and spiritual exemplar
for a wholly unprecedented ideal of a restored Israel through the making of a covenant between the king and the heavenly Sophia.

Could a certain faction of postexilic Jews with connections to Egypt
have revised the very eschatological significance of divine kingship in Israel, renouncing the old Davidic model that seemed to have been dis-
credited during the Babylonian captivity and advancing under the cover

of an "ancient" body of literature attributable to Solomon, but also closely allied with the apocalyptic writings of the desert communities, *a revolutionary movement within Judaism?*

Could the Christian movement at its inception have been less a relatively minor fringe gathering of the disaffected around a rural preacher, as common opinion holds, than an insurrection staged by a well-recognized cadre of traditional Jews who had been out of power since the Roman occupation, but who commanded some real allegiance in the countryside, in the wilderness strongholds, and in the Diaspora?

Could the extent of this cadre's influence been the real reason that Jesus was reviled and hated by the Pharisees, and why he was ultimately framed by the authorities who strove to put him to death? Could an understanding of who this cadre might have been—let us for right now call them the Sophians, who later were known as Nazarenes—disclose a deeper and more common origin for those among the faithful who today regard themselves respectively as Jews and Christians?

Could Jesus' "kingdom not of this world" have been "Solomon's" kingdom, the kingdom of Sophia? Could Jesus himself have set his face toward Jerusalem and overthrow the Davidic rulers and proprietors of the Jerusalem Temple in order to establish this already-anticipated eschatological kingship?

Jesus as Wisdom in the Gospels

Surprisingly, certain major clues that support this hypothesis can be found in the Gospels themselves, especially the incidents surrounding Jesus' encounter with the Jerusalem authorities, along with his arrest and trial on an assortment of specious charges. For instance, there is the following, somewhat perplexing, passage in Matthew, which has often caused trouble for traditional scholars:

> Turning to the assembled Pharisees Jesus asked them, "What is your opinion about the Messiah? Whose son is he?" "The son of David," they replied. "How then is it," he asked, "that David by inspiration calls him 'Lord'? For he says, 'The Lord said to my Lord, "Sit at my right hand until I put your enemies under your feet."' If David calls him 'Lord,' how can he be David's son?" Not a man could say a word in reply; and from that day forward no one dared ask him another question. (Matt. 22:41–46)

A footnote in the *New English Bible* offers the following explanation: "While the story may represent a stratum of tradition which rejected a Son of David Christology, that cannot have been the intention of the evangelist, in light, e.g., of chs. 1–2," which deals with Jesus' genealogy and the Nativity.[38]

Yet, as we have already argued, the first two chapters of Matthew actually raise suspicions about the traditional "Son of David Christology." Rather than inserting some alien "stratum of tradition," the New Testament authors and compilers most likely included this passage as a clue to the meaning of the messianic pageant that was about to unfold before the reader.

One has only to consider the next passage, in which "Jesus then addressed the people and his disciples in these words: 'The doctors of the law and the Pharisees sit in the chair of Moses; therefore do what they tell you; pay attention to their words. But do not follow their practice; for they say one thing and do another' " (Matt. 23:1–3).

A few lines later Jesus also warns the people not to call the Pharisees "rabbi," because "you have one Rabbi, and you are all brothers." "Nor must you be called 'teacher'; you have one Teacher, the Messiah" (Matt. 23:8,10).

The notion of messiah as Teacher corresponds with the wisdom tradition, and Jesus in this section of the Gospel contrasts such a doctrine with the false instruction of the Pharisees, who rely exclusively on the Law of Moses.

It is not, of course, that the Law of Moses itself is false. It is just not properly discerned. It is seen only from the outside, rather than from the inside. The Law, or Torah, can only be taken to heart and comprehended through wisdom. Jesus himself contradicts the Pharisaic notion that the Messiah must be the Son of David, and hence the regal upholder of the Law of Moses, because the Messiah is a greater power on both heaven and earth than any Davidic king might be.

The Messiah is not the Son of God, as the Davidic tradition called him. He is the Son of Man, the messianic name for the One expected by the Sophians!

Jesus is recorded as having made the same distinction, in a slightly veiled manner, when he is cross-examined at his trial by the Sanhedrin prosecutors.[39] The High Priest declares, "By the living God I charge you to tell us: Are you the Messiah, the Son of God?" But Jesus, who has refused to answer the questions of the prosecution directly all along, simply replies, "The words are yours," or "It is as you say," which can be interpreted to mean, "if that is what you mean by the title of messiah." But Jesus then boldly states, "But I tell you this: from now on, you will see the Son of Man seated at the right hand of God and coming on the clouds of heaven" (Matt. 26: 63–64).

Matthew then notes that this testimony made the High Priest furious, who cries "Blasphemy!" and finally appears to have found the one statement of Jesus that would convict him of the highest religious crime. "Need we call further witnesses?" the prosecutor asks. "You have heard the blasphemy. What is your opinion?" The reply: "He is guilty . . . ; he should die" (Matt. 26: 65–66).

Curiously, very few Biblical exegetes have ever asked the nagging question: Why could Jesus have been convicted of a capital crime for suggesting that he was the Son of Man rather than the Son of God?

It is evident from the context that Jesus is not in trouble with the authorities simply for claiming Messiahship. It is the kind of messiahship he seems to be appropriating to his mission. The Roman government was not interested in Jesus' crime because he was not contesting the imperial administration.

But the Sanhedrin had every reason to be obsessed with Jesus, because he was directly challenging the temple cult itself, presided over by Mosaic ideologues, on behalf of the Sophianic vision of divine kingship and Israel's salvation.

As Matthew makes clear, it was Jesus' remarks about destroying the Temple—rather than anything he might have said about the Law itself, or about messianic pretensions to the throne of David, which would have been a simple matter of laughable "credentials" as far as the Sanhedrin were concerned—that sealed his fate with the religious officialdom of his day.

Jesus was in truth a dangerous revolutionary, not so much before Herod and the Roman occupation forces as in the sight of the ancient regime of Davidic Judaism!

Another key to how Jesus viewed himself can be discovered in the series of passages beginning with Luke 18:31, which have been captioned his "Challenge to Jerusalem." We must remember that Jerusalem was David's city, and it certainly would not have been reasonable to expect a claimant to the throne of David to bring his revolutionary agenda to climax by assaulting all the royal traditions and trappings of priestly prerogative associated for a millennium with that city.

The laying waste of Jerusalem by the legions of Nebuchadnezzar more than five centuries earlier had shaken the legacy of Davidic kingship at its core, and Jesus' prophecies of a reenactment of those devastating events, with the Romans now playing the part of the Babylonians, would make no sense if he as "messiah" merely wanted to elevate the connotations of the phrase "Son of David" to a more spiritual altitude.

As it turns out, Jesus himself declares that eschatological challenge to Jerusalem will come from the "Son of Man," who will be rejected and mistreated (Luke 18:31–32) and "on the third day he will rise again" (Luke 18:33). If Jesus were heading for Jerusalem to declare himself king in the traditional sense, it would have been apparent to the disciples what he was up to.

But the Gospel writer demurs that the disciples "understood nothing of all this; they did not grasp what he was talking about; its meaning was concealed from them" (Luke 18:34). There was no formal or ceremonial script for the Son of Sophia to play in the minds of the common people as the culmination of the ascent to eschatological kingship approached.

The playing out of "wisdom" in this context, as Paul would later underscore, was absurd, a folly for the everyday religious imagination. But it was world-shattering, nonetheless.

In the next paragraph Jesus passes on his way through Jericho a blind man who calls out to him, "Jesus, Son of David, have pity on me." Jesus at first treats this entreaty as if it were a kind of annoyance, suggesting that the use of a form of traditional messianic designation meant nothing to the man from Nazareth. It is also pertinent to indicate that belonging to the lineage of David was something the populace seemed to have taken for granted about Jesus, rather than respecting it as a critical title. In fact, only when Jesus realizes that the blind man wants to be healed does he take a serious interest in him (Luke 18:35–42).

Next, we have the tale of Zacchaeus, who tries to catch a furtive glimpse of the Messiah and whom Jesus befriends and into whose home he invites himself, even though the man is a "sinner." Zacchaeus repents of his sins, and Jesus stresses that a forgiven sinner is equally a "son of Abraham," since "the Son of Man has come to seek and save what is lost" (Luke 19:9–10).

Jesus' kingship is one of making Jews again of those who have been disinherited from the promise to Abraham because they have somehow violated the Mosaic code and the Deuteronomic standards of righteousness. The implication of this passage, especially when it is placed in its narrative context, is striking. The Son of Man, Son of Sophia, is not only merciful, but has come to revise radically what is entailed in the traditional concept of "children of the promise."

Being a child of the promise has nothing to do with formal righteousness; it concerns recognizing the true king, savior, and teacher of wisdom and being adopted into his family, which stretches all the way back to Abraham.

The subsequent paragraph, however, sums up the significance of eschatological kingship, which Jesus communicates through a peculiar parable. Luke states that Jesus tells his disciples the parable "because he was now close to Jerusalem and they thought the reign of God might dawn at any moment" (Luke 19:11). It is the parable of "a man of noble birth [who] went on a long journey abroad, to be appointed king and then return" (Luke 19:12).

The parable tells of how the nobleman gives to each of his ten servants a "pound each," instructing them to invest the sum and bring about a significant return. The parable notes that the nobleman's "fellow-citizens hated him, and they sent a delegation on his heels to say, 'We do not want this man as our king'" (Luke 19:14).

When the man returns after having been crowned as king, he finds that not all of his servants have made wise investments. One has squirreled it away out of fear of the nobleman and reaped no return whatsoever. "I was afraid of you," the servant confesses to the master, "because you are a hard man; you draw out what you never put in and reap what you did not sow" (Luke 19:22).

But the master assails the timid steward violently and punishes him by taking away even his meager pound and giving it to the servant who has risked his capital. Then he calls for his enemies to be brought forth and be "slaughtered" in his presence (Luke 19:24–27).

This curious parable has frequently been invoked as a moral tale within the Christian tradition to show approval for stewardship of finances and even, in the age of the robber barons in America, to justify the lack of charity and the economic survival of the fittest.

If one deals with it from a mere ethical standpoint, it seems slightly repugnant, and it contradicts the bulk of Jesus' own recorded moral teachings, particularly those concerning superfluous private wealth and the hoarding of earthly treasures.

But as a historical allusion and cryptic statement about Sophianic kingship, the parable makes perfect sense, especially when viewed in the light of the dramatic sequence of incidents in which it appears. The footnote in the *New English Bible* that says the passage "may be an allusion to some historic incident involving Rome and a member of the Herodian dynasty" is rather silly, and seems to be stretching the point.[40]

The "noble man" who went to be made king is Jesus himself, who is descended from David. His enemies "hate him" and do not want to see him king because they consider him illegitimate, or unworthy, in some way. Their antipathy may have something to do with his reputation as a "hard man" who is neither charitable nor a fair player when it comes to the rules of commerce and industry, as verse 21 emphasizes.

The king who fits this description, of course, was Solomon who, though he was later revered for his wisdom, in his own day was considered a despot who enlarged Israel's power, expanded its glory, and erected a temple through the forced labor of the population and the exaction at times of crushing levies on personal income.

Solomon indeed "drew out what he never put in." His policies were what today we would call capitalistic rather than communitarian. He favored unrestrained trade and exchange of commodities with neighboring states. And it was because of these policies on top of his renowned sexual appetites, military adventures, diplomatic dalliances, and experimentation with foreign religious modalities that the Deuteronomic historians vilified him.

The lesson of the parable at one level is that the legend of the hated king, remembered in actual history for being "hard" and for flouting the Mosaic code, may have something to do with the eschatological moment about to come to pass in Jerusalem.[41] The parable cleverly upsets and reverses, as all Jesus' parables do rhetorically through the Synoptic Gospels, the garden variety approach to things.

It radically revises the accepted notions of the good and morally upright king, who is typically akin to David, while prefiguring the reign of wisdom in which conventional moral platitudes will be upended in favor of the revealing of God's profound secret for the ages. *Freedom from sin is not salvation. Salvation lies in the forgiveness of sins.*

By taking away from the person who has little as the consequence of having done nothing—the Pharisaic version of the righteous individual who does not sin because he risks nothing—the new king sagaciously rewards not those who have not been cautious, godly, and prudent, but who have been faithful to him and heeded his instructions from the beginning.

Their return will be even greater. *Their inheritance is wisdom,* which can only be gained in the marketplace and perhaps even through "prostituting" oneself, as the old myths of Sophia suggest.

The Wisdom of the Cross

By going to Calvary Jesus did not exercise moral restraint, but was humiliated and punished in a manner set aside for society's worst criminals and malefactors.

The wisdom of the cross is still not understood by today's Christian Pharisees, even those with a refined social conscience and a sympathy for the poor and oppressed. It is not understood because it ultimately makes no moral condemnation of those who have broken the code or gone to excess. Perhaps it never will.

A final interpretative key that unlocks the importance of the wisdom tradition can be found in the first chapter of 1 Corinthians where Paul refers to the crucified Jesus as the "power of God" and the "[Sophia] of God" (1 Cor. 1:24).

Here Paul, who is usually maligned by feminists for upholding the patriarchal subjugation of women in his so-called household sayings, is challenging the very patriarchal order of religious belief by identifying Christ with Sophia.

> God has chosen what the world counts weakness. He has chosen things low and contemptible, mere nothings, to overthrow the existing order. . . . You are in Christ Jesus by God's act, for God has made him our [Sophia]; he is our righteousness; in him we are consecrated and set free. (1 Cor. 1:27–30)

The "existing order" is in an important sense the patriarchal order. It is the Davidic order of Judaism, and in the long haul the imperial order of Rome. The kingdom of Christ is the *parousia* of Sophia, of a wisdom hitherto not disclosed to the eyes of humankind.

What it means to be "in Christ," for Paul, is to be part of the New Being and New Wisdom, to be born again through "foolishness" with Sophia. Sophian theology is the true liberation theology. It is to affirm the unity of creation through the disclosure of the true unity of God as both male and female, as high and low, as spirit and body, as word and flesh.

When Jesus in the Gospel of Matthew says he did not come to "abolish, but to complete" the Mosaic Law (Matt. 5:17), he is harking back to the motif of the Wisdom of Sirach in which Sophia is identified with the real Torah.

As emissary of Sophia, Jesus' example on earth constitutes the unveil-ing of what the Law has always signified dimly——mercy and self-giving love, an experience of what God is truly like, the passage from divine shadow to the fulfillment of the promise.[42]

The transcription of the Christian revelation in accordance with the standards of masculine dominion was a slow and gradual process that had to do more with the conditions of Roman society than with the con-tent of the faith itself. The ultimate formulation of orthodox Christian-ity, in which the male Jesus reigned supreme as the fullness of Godhead, came almost four centuries after the death of Jesus, during the time of the church councils when the once young and vital religion had been transformed into a governing instrument of the Roman emperors.

Roman culture was eminently and innately patriarchal. The Ger-manic peoples of Northern Europe who fell heir to the Caesars were even more so. In the meantime the Bible came to be read in Latin, and scholars in the West would not be able to recover the original Greek and Hebrew texts until the sixteenth century. The name "Sophia" disap-peared except in the Eastern church, where she became *Hagia Sophia,* "Saint Sophia," after whom the great church in Constantinople was named.

The foundation of Christian self-knowledge would not have been laid without a sense of the dynamic interaction between the masculine and feminine dimensions of Deity that had prevailed in the ancient Mediter-ranean.

But that foundation remained intact throughout the millennia that followed, including the one that is soon to arrive. Unfortunately, until now, it is a foundation that has been overlooked, but becomes visible as the hard cement of patriarchal illusions cracks and is disassembled.

The very foundation of Christianity and the key to any feminist reread-ing of the tradition, as we shall see, is its own most elemental dogma.

4

The Divine Feminine

*God is love; [whoever] dwells in love is dwelling in
God.*—1 John 4:16, marg.

From the outset the mystery of Christianity has been bound up with the
doctrine of the *divine incarnation.*

The radical edge of this doctrine within ancient—and perhaps the
whole of human—thought has, of course, been blunted over the years
by the cozy familiarity of this particular strand of orthodoxy. Yet on reflection we discover that the idea was very much as puzzling in its own
epoch as it is now. The startling pronouncement in the prologue to the
Gospel of John that the "Word" (Greek, *logos*) became "flesh" through
the humanity of Jesus had a severe shock effect on the attitudes of classical antiquity.

The mythic intuition that the power of the cross on which Jesus was
crucified could somehow reconcile the ways of heaven with the fate of an
unregenerate humanity took centuries to be clarified theologically.

Meanwhile, the idea of a God who became human anticipated the
modern sentiment that what is most divine cannot be separated from the
riddle of daily life. The centerpiece of the early Christian creeds concerning the incarnation was the down-to-earth observation that Jesus was
"born of a woman." More important, it implied that God was directly involved in the birthing process.

But, if Jesus was begotten of woman, it was necessary to take the next
logical step and conclude that God had, unmistakably, made the feminine bestowal of life something utterly sacred. The dogma of Christ's virgin birth left in doubt whether sexual intercourse itself could be regarded as holy, as had often been the case in the paganism of the
Mediterranean basin. But the net result of the Christian revolution in
faith and morals was to hallow family life, and woman's role in it. This
consecration of domestic affairs had not been conceivable in the patriarchal and often brutal society of imperial Rome.

While the feminine principle in ancient religion faded along with the
slow demise of the worship of ancient goddesses, hastened by an outright
ban by church authorities, it returned full force by the sixth century C.E.
with the flowering of the cult of the Virgin Mary.

Religious historians have scratched their heads over the sudden popularity of "Mary worship," just about when Christianity became the official religion of the Roman Empire. It was also the time when the barbarians of Northern Europe were, coup by coup, dragging down the pillars of imperial authority all the way from the boot of Italy to the British Isles. The rapid growth of the virgin cult from the fifth century onward is even more remarkable, because neither the New Testament nor the pronouncements of the early church fathers furnish much of an intellectual justification for Marianism.

The "historical" Mary, mentioned sparingly in the Gospels, is rather nondescript. And, strangely, with the exception of the Nativity passages at the opening of the Gospels of Matthew and Luke, she is portrayed, at worst, as interfering in Jesus' own ministry and, at best, as having an ambiguous relationship with her son. Mary Magdalene, the prostitute, seems to be more beloved by Jesus in the Gospels than the very "womb that bore him."

Students of early Christianity have served up a variety of explanations for the immense appeal of Marianism throughout the Middle Ages, despite its lack of canonical foundations. None of these accounts, however, turns out to be very satisfactory. Some researchers have proposed that devotion to Mary stemmed from the sly appropriation of pagan goddess worship by a triumphal Catholic Church. But this theory ignores the fact that paganism was by and large defunct by the end of the fourth century.

Others have speculated that there had always been a highly secretive, and "heretical," cult of Jesus' mother, persisting from the days of the first apostles. According to this argument, such a cult finally came out of the closet when Catholicism was sufficiently strong and diverse to tolerate such thinking. Known to the bishops of the fourth century as the Collyridians, this cult supposedly was a "dissident body" made up mostly of women, who gave their primary allegiance not to Jesus, but to the Virgin and Queen of Heaven, "a form of the goddess."[1]

Such arguments are weakened by the historical observation that the heyday of heresy *preceded* the consolidation of the Roman Catholic religion in the Western empire. They also suffer from a failure to see that by the time Marianism was at high tide, church power was also nearing its zenith.

The third version of what went on during this period is even more problematic. This explanation, which draws heavily from psychoanalysis and Jungian psychology, maintains that Western Christianity—dominated after the fourth century by Latin bishops and clergy from the Germanic tribes, both of which groups were patriarchal to the extreme in their morals and values—was merely "compensating" through its collective beliefs for the low status accorded in real life to women.

Such an analysis seems attractive, because it reinforces modern social scientific views that human beings will contrive in their imaginations whatever is absent in their everyday experience. But the social scientific standpoint, which tends to build on generalizations drawn from limited historical data, overlooks the obvious conclusion that there have been eras, such as King David's Israel, when intense patriarchal piety did *not* allow for the expression of any feminist alternative within the official tradition.

One could surely make the case that after the feminine side of God has been repressed for generations, it will find strategic ways of wending its way back into religious consciousness. Nevertheless, the theory is too pat. And it makes little sense of the trend in the High Middle Ages toward exalting Mary even above God the Son and God the Father. The trend developed side by side with the deep-rooted misogynist prejudice fomented by the church of the time regarding the inherent lustfulness, moral inferiority, and general depravity of the female sex.

The problem with so much of what has been written or surmised over the years about the Virgin Mary is that it treats what is largely a religious dilemma as a question of social construction or pure human invention. Because we are so influenced nowadays by psychological and anthropological thinking about the character of religion, we refuse to acknowledge that religious changes may be somewhat *sui generis,* all the while insisting that there must be some mundane set of reasons for what is happening at a cosmic or supernatural level.

We find it difficult to entertain the possibility that the divine voice itself may speak with a gendered or engendering inflection. Because modern scholarship has spent so much time undermining the credibility of patriarchal traditions through a critique of male-contoured social institutions, it has come to assume that social institutions themselves somehow always can be cited to explicate religious matters.

Social scientific reasoning repeatedly commits in its own way the logical fallacy of what is known as *post hoc ergo propter hoc*—if x follows y, then y must be the cause of x. The emerging voice of woman today in the arena of faith may have little to do in causal terms with the social and political emancipation of females during recent generations.

The two developments may be virtually concurrent. They may be in themselves a powerful signaling of *divine agency*—the action of the Two in One in contemporary time and space.

The same may be true with earlier eruptions of the divine feminine in human history. Religious scholarship rarely assumes that the appeal of the first apostles throughout Roman society was due merely to the prospects of a new, Jewish paternalism available to the downtrodden Mediterranean masses.

For the same reason, it is silly to suppose that Marianism grew because it somehow rectified the social and psychological balance during the dark centuries from the collapse of Rome to the rise of modern Europe. In fact, the phenomenon of Marian enthusiasm was only a segment of a broader, but relatively less chronicled, spectacle of deep, religious changes taking place between 500 and 1350 C.E.

The real spiritual force behind the adoration of Mary during the Dark Ages was the dim recognition in the maw of a patriarchal culture that femininity was indispensable to divinity.

Much of the modern effort to psychologize the Marian tradition has wrongly paid attention to the asexuality of "God's mother." But the myth of Mary may have more to do with sexuality than we suspect.

The story of Jesus' conception in the Synoptic Gospels dwells on the "union" of an earthly woman and the Holy Spirit. The doctrine of the incarnation requires a marvelous interpenetration between the transcendent powers of heaven and the organs of generation.

For Jesus to be "born of a woman," the female anatomy, and the fact of sexuality, must be affirmed in an entirely new manner.

This profound insight can be extracted from the Nativity tale itself. The nature of the divine union with an actual woman is so much like ordinary conjugal lovemaking that Joseph, to whom Mary is betrothed, believes his wife may have become pregnant through an illicit liaison. "Being a man of principle, and at the same time wanting to save [Mary] from exposure, Joseph desired to have the marriage contract set aside quietly" (Matt. 1:19).

In short, the belief in the Virgin Mary reinforced the paradoxical concept of the incarnation. It made sexuality and the bringing forth of life something that had a holiness that signified far more than the orgiastic rounds of enjoyment and ecstasy in ancient paganism.

It is not at all coincidental that medieval statuary of Mary focuses on the intimate bonding between *mother and child*. The *epopteia* of the Eleusian mysteries allegedly had unveiled the mystery that the "maiden" gives birth to a divine child, who harbors the secret of immortality.

Woman is the bearer of life eternal. She is the first witness to the incarnation. That is the gift of Sophia, or Mary as she was called during a different historical era.

The Troubadors

But at the end of the Dark Ages there also dawned an awareness that passionate human love—the love between men and women—might also have its own kind of sacrality. This discovery went hand in hand with a dramatic transformation of European culture itself.

In 1099 C.E. French knights, at the instigation of Pope Urban II, marched on and sacked Jerusalem in the name of the cross of Christ as part of the First Crusade. Within a century the Knights Templars had been instituted as a fighting order of religious celibates to guard the highways and protect the pilgrims on their way to Jerusalem.

A modest French author named Chrétien de Troyes crafted in literary form for the first time the saga of King Arthur, the Round Table, and the quest for the Holy Grail—the legendary jeweled cup in which the blood of Christ had been kept and which supposedly offered salvation for any knight who might attain the chalice.[2]

Meanwhile, the monk St. Bernard at the monastery of Clairvaux, who had exhorted and commended the Templars for their heroic deeds, began to compose fiery and none-too-veiled erotic commentaries on the Song of Songs while advancing the ideal that the Christian's love for God was not unlike the desire of a swain for his mistress. Bernard himself also promoted the ideal of the warrior monk and the selfless quest for the Grail as the supreme object of desire.[3]

And in Southern France, in the region called Languedoc or Provence, a new breed of poets and musicians known as troubadours popularized the concept of *romantic love,* extolling the beauty of women and rhapsodizing over the suffering of suitors in pursuit of the dangerous goal of sexual intercourse with a married lady.[4]

Today the twelfth century seems both alien and faraway from us. Its genuine literary remains have been altered many times over as the stuff of chivalric fantasy and Victorian novelettes. Yet it was also an age in which the call of the divine feminine had reached a crescendo.

Western culture was on the verge of a transformation into what we regard as a modern sensibility with its emphasis on the importance of individual lives and the fulfillment of personal desire. The catalyst for these cultural changes, curiously enough, seems to have been the troubadour movement.

Nowadays the controversy over who the troubadours were, and what they did, has been generally forgotten. We remember them mainly as vagrant minstrels and lyric poets whose verses helped craft the vernacular tongues of what would later become the separate nations of Europe.

The troubadours are best known for having created a ripe and highly popular genre of medieval love poetry, reviving interest in such secular and religiously scandalous classic authors as Ovid and paving the way for the unabashed secularism and sensuality of the Italian Renaissance. But they also had a slightly veiled "theological" agenda, which contemporary admirers are only beginning to figure out.

Troubadour sensibility, of course, frequently becomes confused with the mysterious doctrines of a group of twelfth-century heretics in Southern France known simultaneously as Cathars and Albigensians.

The origin of the word "Cathar" is obscure. The name "Albigensian" is taken from the town name Albi, where the heresy flourished. The Cathars themselves apparently referred to themselves as the *perfecti,* "completed ones." The large majority of them were killed, and their religion destroyed, in the first part of the thirteenth century when the pope ordered the same crusading knights who had captured Jerusalem for the glory of Western Christendom to attack the Albigensian strongholds and put to death countless men, women, and children in the name of rescuing the Holy Catholic Church from its internal enemies.[5]

The troubadours, some of whom were actual eyewitnesses to and recorders in epic stanzas of the Albigensian wars, came to be associated with the heretics for several major reasons.

First, the troubadours had the misfortune of coming from the same basic stratum of society as the Cathars, which was fiercely anticlerical and anti-Roman in its politics.

Second, the troubadours' glorification of extramarital love affairs and their dalliances in the castles of noblewomen gave them a not undeserved reputation for libertinism and questionable behavior, connected in the average person's mind with religious heresy.

Third, it is clear that many aristocratic ladies who sponsored the troubadours were probably also Cathar sympathizers, even if they were not actual practitioners of the heresy.

However, the association was on the main coincidental. For Provence was in its own right not unlike the California of several decades ago—an economically booming region with a mild climate near the seacoast where all sorts of radical new ideas and styles of cultural experimentation were not only allowed but encouraged. Just as California by its own chemistry produced both peaceful hippies and violent cultists such as Charles Manson, both of whom were reviled by the society at large, so the environment of Languedoc gave rise to religious purists and would-be promoters of a sexual revolution that may, in retrospect, have been more talk than actual historical trend.

The differences between the Albigensians and the troubadours were quite striking. The heretics viewed themselves as sincere practitioners of early, apostolic Christianity. They lived simply and frugally, refrained from the ostentatious dress and show of luxury in which the monastic orders of the time indulged, and counseled sexual abstinence of their followers.

Their quarrel with the Roman Church was quite similar to the fight between the Catholics and the supporters of Martin Luther and John Calvin some four centuries later. They have sometimes been seen as perceived "proto-Protestants," pressing the same volley of complaints as the Reformers against the clergy's abuse of religious authority, its worldliness, and its excesses.

The comparison is not at all precise, because the Albigensians did not uphold the supreme truth of scripture, as did the Protestants. Furthermore, they fell under suspicion from the establishment because they held to a not uncommon Near Eastern, but far from Christian, system of beliefs often referred to as Manicheanism, or dualism, after the Persian prophet Mani who founded a sect by that name.

Both Manicheans and Albigensians thought that the goodness of God did not necessarily triumph over the forces of evil in the universe, and that the cross of Christ could not really save anybody from suffering or damnation. These sorts of speculations really bore little in common with the troubadours who were playful, sexually suggestive, and unconcerned with the broad metaphysical picture.

Catharism was in considerable measure a pessimistic religious philosophy that appealed to the disenfranchised and the disgruntled. The troubadour spirit centered on the highly optimistic idea that, as we say, "love conquers all," or that love alone is the one redeeming power in the cosmos.

This notion that, in order to find fulfillment in life, "all you need is love," permeates modern popular culture. But it was an exceedingly radical precept during its own era.

The exaltation of the notion of "salvation by love alone" is still by most standards rather arguable, even in this day and age. But it was also the context for a strongly detectable upsurge in awareness of what can only be called the divine feminine.

Courtly Love

Whereas so many medieval historians have been preoccupied with the official cult of the Virgin that flourished about the same time as the troubadours, scarcely little attention has been directed toward the deep-reaching and very serious *religious* implications of the troubadour teachings themselves.

It is even possible that church patronage of Marian devotion during the Middle Ages can be construed as an effort to co-opt at an official level, and to chasten, the already pervasive cultural sympathies for the divine feminine that had been set in motion by the troubadours, who were quite influential across Europe. This explanation is more plausible historically than psychological theories touting the need for collective spiritual balance between the energies and archetypes of male and female.

The troubadour concept of love, and the attendant ideal of exalted womanhood, is not at all as feudal and patronizing of women as has sometimes been suspected. Much of our understanding of medieval romance has been colored by the values and tastes of the nineteenth century, which rediscovered the artistic allure and spiritual attractiveness of knightly heroism and chivalry.

The incredible popularity of Richard Wagner's operas, which gave a heavily baroque and highly Germanic twist to the original medieval stories, have had a lasting effect too on the perceptions of troubadour poetry. Wagner's *Tristan und Isolde* is a marvelous total art work of the Victorian era, but those characters bear less relation than most suspect to the adulterous lovers of the Dark Ages.

What, then, were the underlying themes of the troubadour movement that have enduring significance? The principal theme concerned the elegant and beautiful lady to whom the troubadour gave his heart, and for whom he was willing to suffer, not just extensively, but often unjustly.

The vision of love, not only as ennobling but as salvific, can be found in the lines of the Gascony troubadour Marcabru (1129–1150 C.E.).

Marcabru is remembered for having castigated the frivolous and lustful sentiments of many of his fellow troubadours, and for having subtly transmuted the medieval language of divine love into a celebration of eternal bonding between men and women.

Male and female adoration, or "good love," says Marcabru, is equivalent in both moral and spiritual scope to love of one's neighbor, *agapē* in Greek, *caritas,* "charity," in Latin. People are made whole through "one single longing of two desires, in trust that is firm, . . . precious, true pure." For

> Love has the meaning
> of emerald and sard,
> it is the top and root of Joy,
> it is a lord who rules with truth,
> and its power overcomes every creature.
> By its word, its action, and its look,
> it comes from a true heart
> when it gives its promise and pledge—
> if only it does not befoul its gifts;
> and whoever does not hasten to it
> bears the name of fool.[6]

For the most part, the troubadours changed the orthodox Christian ethic of taking up the cross and suffering for God's kingdom into the idea of undergoing endless grief for the affection of a lady. As Blondel de Nesle, who lived during the second half of the twelfth century in Northern France where he would technically have been called a *trouvère* rather than a troubadour, sang of his desired lady:

> If she knew all about
> my martyrdom and disease—
> if she for whom I let Love
> hold me and work me till I am weak, new,
> Then I believe she would send
> relief without delay;
> for that's what she ought to do by right
> unless that deliberate look
> in her beautiful eyes is a lie.[7]

Love, for Blondel, is indeed "martyrdom." The troubadour agonizes for the lady's holy and "virtuous" love. The singer asks that his entire life be given over to her, and that she take his body and soul upon her in her mercy.

Yet the saintly suffering of the troubadour depends on the disinterest and caprice on the part of the beautiful one. The more she ignores or despises him, which she usually did because she was a married woman of high birth who could only tryst with the troubadour in shame and secrecy, the more his own love is inflamed and made a religious passion. According to Thibaut de Champagne,

> Love has great power, great force
> which makes you search things out without reason, at her pleasure.[8]

The basic rule of courtly love is laid out by Andreas Capellanus in his dialogue titled "On Love." Love, writes Capellanus, "is an inborn suffering which results from the sight of, and uncontrolled thinking about, the beauty of the other sex. This feeling makes a man desire before all else the embrace of the other sex, and to achieve the utter fulfillment of the commands of love in the other's embrace by their common desire."[9]

Although some commentators have portrayed the type of courtly love praised by the troubadours as the yearning of commoner men for women of high status, Capellanus's argument makes it plain that the social positions of lover and beloved are irrelevant. The point is that heterosexual love is a form of divine love that has not been grasped by the human intellect. For instance, there is a passage in Capellanus where "a man of higher nobility" addresses a commoner in terms befitting of both a noblewoman and a heavenly figure.

The nobleman says that he has set his "whole mind's purpose and anchor in" the love for the woman. Without that love,

> no worldly possession seems to me worth having, and abundance of all worldly things I regard as the height of poverty. Your love alone would crown me with a king's diadem, and endow me with abundance of all riches in the greatest material poverty. The hope of your love keeps me alive in this world, and if my hopes of you are dashed, I must take leave from life. So I pray that in your kindness you may deign to preserve me for your service, and not reject the love of a count. . . . In your wisdom, then, you should reflect on the faith and devotion of this count who addresses you, and repay him with a reply worthy of his merits.[10]

The conventional view of courtly love has been that it was completely secular in its intent and that it consisted of highly ritualized, and by extension not quite serious, kinds of give-and-take between the sexes. The same view holds that courtly love was a passing cultural fashion that took flight at a historically unique moment of knightly gallantry, social tension, and moral permissiveness.

According to this perspective, the customs of courtly love remain an enigma to us and can no more be assimilated to contemporary habits of thought than mythic dragons and wizards.

Yet it is evident from even a casual study of the courtly poetry of the twelfth century that a powerful form of religious fervor was in the making. In much of the poetry Marian devotion intermingles, both naturally and self-consciously, with barely concealed erotic rhapsodies about desiring stolen kisses and clandestine rendezvous with earthly lady loves.

Could the familiar hymns and hallowings of Jesus' mother, which long ago acquired orthodox acceptance in world Catholicism, be quite intimately connected with the praises of real women? And might some renewed "archaeology" of the courtly love traditions give us some important, if not profound, biographical information about the female side of the Godhead?

Sophia and Songs of Love

The troubadour doctrine of salvation by love is not as "off-line" and "un-canonical" as either the church of its time or modern critics have tended to suggest.[11] The theme recurs throughout the wisdom literature of the Bible, and is exemplified most dramatically in the passage from the Song of Songs where love is described as "strong as death" and the anonymous author proclaims, "Many waters cannot quench love, no flood can sweep it away" (Song of Songs 8:6–7).

The Song of Songs is about the divine call of desire. It represents the beginnings of a rich but concealed theology within postexilic Judaism related to the rise of Sophian thinking that probably became an important strand within primitive Christianity. The parables of Jesus recorded in the Synoptic Gospels about the virgins who keep their lamps lit, awaiting the appearance of the "bridegroom," have strong resonances with the Song of Songs and reflect some kind of implicit, but familiar, eschatological myth about the ultimate appearance of God in history as a "wedding ceremony" between "woman" and "man."

The last chapter of the book of Revelation in which the faithful are summoned to the "marriage" of the "bride" and the "Lamb" is a powerful, and symbolically charged, declaration of what may have been basic Christian eschatology all along. The desert tradition within Judaism of a "spiritual marriage with Sophia" may have been the foundation itself of such an eschatology.

Indeed, Sophianism itself, with its emphasis on the manifestation within time of the "true" body/temple could very well have been, as we have already seen, the tacit force in both Judaism and Christianity behind the repeated waves of eschatological enthusiasm. The undertones of erotic union within this eschatology are also unmistakable.

By the end of the Dark Ages Sophian eschatology had for the most part established itself within both Eastern Christianity and the Muslim-dominated religiosity of Turkey and Palestine. The mysterious figure of St. Sophia, after whom the great church in Constantinople is named, testifies to this legacy. It is interesting that both the Marian revival in Latin Christendom and the fame of the troubadours coincided with the movement west of the Frankish crusaders and their eventual contact, after a hiatus of about five centuries, with this heritage.

It has been argued that both the worship of Mary during the High Middle Ages and the courtly love sensibility had their origins in the East, in the region the Crusaders called *Outremer* (literally, "beyond the sea")—that is, the Levant and to a certain extent the Byzantine provinces themselves.

Since time immemorial the East had been the kingdom of the Great Mother, the land at the rising of the sun where the divine feminine had been a pervasive religious influence and had worn countless masks from the Egyptian Isis to the Phrygian Cybele. Now the divine feminine found its way west once more and invaded the dogmatic fortresses of Germanic Christianity.

The fact that Sophia became the lady in the troubadour idiom and the Mother of God in Catholic piety is not as problematic as it may look on the surface.[12] Conventional religious history has proposed that the Mary of the Middle Ages amounted collectively to the old pagan goddesses of Europe redivivus.

But this seemingly commonsense interpretation falters at one critical level. The heavenly woman of the Western imagination from the eleventh century forward was no longer the mistress of childbirth, sexual attraction, crops, and the birth of animals, although she certainly continued to wear that kind of disguise in predominantly peasant societies. She was now primarily an exemplar of both physical and spiritual beauty.

She was a representation of *woman as personality* independent of the female's biological and procreative functions. She was the mysterious and holy Sophia. She was loved in her own right and for her own sake. Gender, as opposed to simple biology, now engulfed the religious vision of the West.

The Development of Sophia

It is this hitherto undisclosed Sophian subtext to the cultural history of the West that forges the link between the sacred and profane aspects of the religious Renaissance that took place about the time of the commercial expansion of Europe and the onset of the Crusades. It also tends to illuminate what have been viewed previously as inexplicable or disconnected social patterns and shifts. For instance, the troubadours' preoccupation with the elegant and distant lady in the walled castle and their advocacy of clandestine, adulterous affairs as a form of almost religious ecstasy does not have to be seen simply as a countercultural or antinominian kind of protest against feudal morality and the corruption of the Roman Church.

Nor must it be regarded as just one more incident of artistic exoticism and decadence that plagues a wealthy ruling class at any given juncture in the annals of humanity. As a fundamental and unprecedented revolutionary flash of change in the conventions of religious signification, troubadour imagery served to liberate the sense of what values shone most brightly in the constellation of the divine feminine. It expelled from religious consciousness the childish fixation on the succoring mother to an emergent feeling for the adult mystique of womanhood.

The "lady in the tower" was something much more than a rarefied object of sexual compulsion, because she held a distinctive power over men that neither mothers nor wives enjoyed. What philosophers would call a dialectical movement had, almost unnoticed, taken place in the religious mind. The ancient spell that bound the numinous appreciation of the feminine to the cycles of birth and death, marriage and childbearing, had suddenly been broken.

Troubadour dalliance had the main effect of spiritually and psychologically challenging the concept that what was most "holy" about woman was her fixed position within the biological family.

In effect, both courtly love and Catharism ritualized an emerging mood of rebellion against the old Greco-Roman structure of misogynist repression, continued by the Latin church, which had been based on the view that the purpose of women is to breed for the preservation of family and state. Both the courtiers and the Cathars preached love as the absolute personal obligation, and both may have sympathized with each other's agenda in some sense.

When the Cathar heretics contended that holy matrimony was nothing else than consecrated whoredom, they were evoking the kind of religious radicalism that proved destructive in the short run, but eventually led to a new evaluation of what women actually are in both earth and heaven.

The medieval Catholic Church was never, of course, happy with the cultural alchemy that was pushing toward an exaltation of the status of women. Catholic doctrine and ecclesiastical administration were Roman in origin, which is to say they were patriarchal. The preeminence of the male-run, medieval monastery was a Latin innovation.

At the same time as the troubadours were honing the ethic of courtly love, Cisterician monks in France under the leadership of Bernard of Clairvaux were developing an allegorical or antisexual reading of sacred love poetry, focused on the Song of Songs.

The spread of Grail mythology may also be related to this trend. The Grail is what in rhetoric is called a metonym—the substitution of a related term for the actual thing—within the language of divine love. It is a metonym for Mary without her sexuality. It is the "lady" symbolically transmuted into a mysterious inanimate object, the acquisition of which demands self-denial and chastity.

The Grail is associated in the religious mind with blood, with the "sacred heart," with the rose, with forbidden desire and a "distancing" of oneself from a dark beauty.[13] It is all of these passions disguised and concealed to themselves in the sublimation of the erotic in the service of immortality and eternal wisdom.

The beloved in this setting became God, or Jesus, or Mary herself. Bernard wrote his own spiritual encomiums to Lady Charity with all the rhetorical trappings but none of the erotic insinuations of the troubadours. One should discipline the entirety of one's physical desires, according to Bernard, as the soul ascends through love toward God.

Only God, who is the alpha and omega of human loving, can truly "satisfy the spirit." That indeed was the entire purpose of the monastery itself, to regiment minds and bodies for the yearning of eros toward the supernatural source of bliss.[14]

Once the Albigensian crusade, which Bernard heartily supported, had been successfully and brutally brought to conclusion, orthodox thought reflected more readily the monastic conception. Meanwhile, the troubadour spirit had been almost entirely extinguished, while the new and improved version of Marianism took up much of the slack.

As feminist historian Marina Warner observes, the Virgin Mary now became "an establishment prop." For "by interfusing the ethic sung by the poets of courtly love with the ancient adherence of the Church to sexual chastity and female submission," the danger of Mary being used as an icon of feminine autonomy had been waylaid, and her worship "could be deftly woven into the fabric of patriarchal politics."[15]

Bernardianism was victorious. The Virgin Mother became a plaster icon. She was turned into an example of how to subjugate natural human desires to the morality of the celibate orders, who held higher status in the church's view than the laity. But, in point of fact, she remained a *mother*—the crowning glory of womanhood.[16]

With respect to the history of the emancipation of the female spirit, Marianism was a backsliding. The troubadours, for all their verbal flamboyance that might well today be called chauvinistic, were highly solicitous of the dignity of women. Their romance of "the lady" was more than exhibitionism. It was the first shot fired in a millennial war for the deployment and control of religious symbols.

The tradition of courtly love, whether deliberately or not, injected into Western Christian thought key elements of the wisdom and mystery religions. The chief contribution of the troubadours, of course, was a highly stylized poetics and the use of literary emotion that would not be duplicated until the nineteenth century.

Despite recurring speculation that the troubadours may have guarded or passed along certain mystical "secrets" in their communications, the evidence is strong that they were mainly artists and musicians, not seers.

On the other hand, the method of the troubadours was always to veil or to obscure, as they did their intrigues with women. They were forerunners of what the Danish philosopher Søren Kierkegaard in the nineteenth century would term the style of "indirection"—the production of semblances, the deliberate fomenting of contradictory impressions or paradoxical sentences.[17]

The typical troubadour opening to a lengthy rhyme was to jar the expectations of the listener. For example, Guillaume IX intones, "My companions, I am going to make a *vers* that is refined, and it will have more foolishness than sense."[18] Marcabru begins, "I say he's a wise man . . . who makes out, word for word, what my song signifies."[19]

The versifier is deliberately speaking in "parables" or riddles, which is common within the ancient wisdom tradition. The impact is for the troubadour to undercut the routine and commonsensical presuppositions of his audience and to invite deep reflection. The courtly lyric has the form of a polished address within a hierarchical order of social relations and cultural signs.

Yet its intended effect is to disrupt that order. The habitual complaint of some contemporary debunkers of the history of medieval courtiers that they did not in reality engage in scandalous affairs to the extent that their own rhetoric and reputation would indicate thus becomes irrelevant. The language of courtly love is transgressive as well as revelatory, like the parables of the Synoptic Gospels and the apocalyptic writers of the Old Testament.

It is meant to confound for the sake of undraping a higher wisdom, the wisdom that is attained in an understanding of what the Christian doctrine of incarnation *must* by its own context and logic encapsulate— the union of masculine and feminine, the alliance of the spirit and the body, and the veritable fusion of divine love and human desire.

It is certainly plausible to presuppose that such an insight occurred to faithful devotees and theological thinkers long before the twentieth century. The problem was that this Sophian kind of religious reflection was generally not possible under Roman orthodoxy, which drew on the grammar of law and imperial politics to forge what later would be regarded as the common creeds of Western Christendom.

It was not even possible at the height of the Protestant Reformation, which simply turned Roman scholasticism on its head and replaced the legalism of the canon doctors with the literalism of scriptural authority. Neither John Calvin nor Martin Luther was capable of grasping the "philo-sophical" import of Jesus' parables, or the apocalyptic works that they went so far as to disregard, as their opponents were equipped to figure out what they had in mind with the teaching of justification by faith.

Sophia and the Knights Templars

What seems to have happened is that the Sophian subtext of Western culture did not merely go underground, but somehow was distorted and sectioned off in its own weird way as what certain enthusiasts would wrongly regard as a secret tradition.

The notion of a Sophian secret has been bound up for centuries with the lore, legends, and rites surrounding the medieval Knights Templars.

The Templars, established in 1118 as a military order sworn to defend the lives and property of Christian pilgrims traveling to the Holy Land in the wake of the First Crusade and the Holy Sepulcher, were disbanded by Pope Clement V in 1312 through the machinations of King Philip IV (the Fair) of France.[20] At the same time, their leadership was tortured and killed, on charges of having harbored vile heresies and practiced sexual deviancy and sodomy.[21] They were also accused of secretly worshiping a mysterious idol known as Baphomet.

By the nineteenth century the Templars had become lionized as powerful magicians and remembered, especially within the Masonic fraternities, as heroes of a kind of covert faith. The accusations brought by Philip's inquisitors against the Templars, most of which were probably either trumped up or outright fabricated, came to be preserved ironically as the substance of the ancient mysteries they allegedly vouchsafed.

But these mysteries may, in fact, have a recognizable origin. The principal indictment against the Templars was that they worshiped Baphomet, to whom they swore loyalty. The name Baphomet has been the subject of voluminous speculation, much of which has been vaporized by silly sorts of linguistic or historical inferences. Some scholars have speculated that the word was a corruption of the name Mahomet, although this argument is weakened by the realization, then as well as now, that Muslims do not bow before idols.

Others have proposed that Baphomet was a Near Eastern word for some kind of pagan fertility deity, but that possibility is preempted by the fact that the Templars probably obtained their "heresy," if that is what it can be termed, through contact with the highly sophisticated culture of thirteenth-century Islam. It is unlikely that either Arabs or Turks by that time were reverting to the wild ceremonies of their Mediterranean peasant predecessors.

The one hypothesis that does ring true, controversial though it may be, is that the name Baphomet was really a cryptogram for Sophia.[22] If the Templar secret was actually some rendition of the Sophian mystery, which probably came to them through Eastern Orthodoxy from Constantinople, many of the scattered and inscrutable pieces of the unsolved Templar puzzle finally begin to fit together.

First, the Sophian tradition that was as old as the legends surrounding Solomon and Jesus may have been preserved throughout the Dark Ages in a form that later could have been twisted and construed by the church as a singular type of heresy. Both the Knights Templars and the troubadours took the dove as their chief symbol.[23] The dove, of course, was also the ancient symbol of Sophia.

In Christian orthodoxy the dove signified the Holy Spirit. But the peculiar use of this symbol in the twelfth and thirteenth centuries, as well as the ubiquitous spread in art and architecture of such other Sophian emblems as the rose, may very well indicate that many among the orthodox also recognized that the Trinitarian concept of the Holy Spirit hinged upon an ancient appreciation for the feminine side of the Godhead.

Second, the Knights Templars were also known as the Knights of the Temple of Solomon. Their primary mission, once Jerusalem had been conquered by the Crusaders at the turn of the twelfth century, was to commandeer the site regarded as the ancient Temple of Solomon and to protect wayfarers and Christian travelers en route to the place.

It is hard to conceive that the Templars did not know about or come in contact with the Sophian lore associated with the Temple of Solomon. While efforts have been made to link the Templars straightaway with the Cathars and with dualism and Gnosticism,[24] the bulk of historical evidence supports the order's own protestation at its trial that the Knights were not heretics.

At minimum, the Templars did not behave as heretics, as did the Cathars, flaunting their differences with the authorities in Rome. It is far more likely that the Templar heresy was actually some discrete version of Sophian Christianity that retained the style of the mystery religions, as it had since the first century.

The Templar secret may have been the revelation to devotees that Christ, as opposed to the historical Jesus, was female as well as male. It may also have been the blasphemy of which they were accused by the Inquisition.

Third, the savage campaigns in the thirteenth and fourteenth centuries of the Frankish kings against the population and culture of Southern France, where Templar strength was greatest, can be better grasped in this context.

Southern France was at the crossroads of the new overseas commerce between the Levant and Europe, and it was a natural locale for what were originally ideas of Eastern Christianity to be seeded, sprout, and take root. Because the fierce and bitter competition between the Western and Eastern empires during the Middle Ages has sometimes been scanted by modern historians, there has been a tendency to ignore the possibility that the schismatic movements which broke out in France and Germany during and after the Crusades could have been inspired as much by a rival wing of historical Christianity as by Gnostic or pagan thought.

The Roman Catholic ecclesiastics of the day despised the troubadour subculture, and also the agenda of the Knights Templars, because the latter bore the "feminist," Sophian views of Christian morality and spirituality, in opposition to the patriarchal and legalistic character of the Western church that had been the norm since the conversion of Constantine.

The Albigensian Crusade during the early thirteenth century and the assault on the Templars in 1307, therefore, are knotted together by the same threads of history. Both events reflect what was apparently a quiet struggle between the monarchs of Northern France, in alliance with the Papacy, and religious revolutionaries afire with notions derived from the heritage of the Middle East and running back to biblical times.

The kings of France fancied themselves champions of Holy Rome, which could be traced back through the emperor Charlemagne to Constantine and ultimately to the apostle Peter. In certain respects, their vision of empire was messianic in the Judaic and Davidic mold. It was a kingdom "of this world," which would guarantee moral and political order *through a savior ruler of the temporal realm*, who would alternately be the pope or monarch.

The medieval belief, for example, that the pope was the vicar of Christ, or vicarious authority for the divine on earth, corresponded in most elements to the Israelite conception of their king as Son of God as well as son of David. The patriarchal force of Jewish-Christianity has always at a structural level developed from this identification of sacred life with sacred kingship.

The Sophian, or Solomonic, legacy out of which primitive Christianity initially sprang, has been quite different. Whereas the Davidic paradigm of the kingdom of God focused on the maintenance of divine law and the paternal regulation of personal, family, and political life over time, the Sophian emphasis was on the protection of the messianic secret by inconspicuous, covenanting groups of equals until the end of time.

An unwillingness to reveal the secret was part of God's plan, which may not look like from the outside what it actually is on the inside. Furthermore, any understanding of the various ciphers, paradoxes, and glyphs that served to encode the meaning of the apocalyptic moment when things hidden to the world would at last be disclosed, required not a mortal mind but divine discernment.

Like the number of the beast in the book of Revelation, such an understanding called for a special kind of "intelligence" associated with the quest for wisdom (Rev. 13:18). The interest of various heretical sects in the material of John's Gospel, where Jesus himself comes across as the chief keeper of secrets, reinforced this tendency.

Hence, Jacques de Molay, the grand master of the Knights Templars who was tortured to death through slow roasting over a fire for his recalcitrance in the face of demands by King Philip IV and the Inquisition that he confess to the abominations and "conspiratorial" aims of the order, could in all honesty vow unto his own death that the brotherhood was not "heretical" in the usual sense of the word.

The premise that this Sophian circle endured down through time in any formal manner is, of course, subject to serious dispute. No scholar has precisely located the so-called Johannine Circle associated with the New Testament literature connected with John, let alone extended such a very plausible theory to include the Sophians.

Sophianism was obviously an underground movement in the West, although it remains unclear as to what degree its partisans were that much out of the mainstream, so far as Eastern Christianity was concerned. The lack of good historical sources that might illuminate the specific odyssey from east to west of the kind of innovative and heretical thought that permeated Southern Europe about the time of the Crusades obscures the picture.

The problem has also been compounded by the presence of a third kind of orthodoxy in the West—Christian hermeticism, esotericism, or occultism—which routinely links the Gnostic Sophia to everything mysterious or rejected by the church from the Middle Ages to the current era. This speculation has become a sort of staple for much of today's feminist religious scholarship. And it posits a "kinder and gentler" tradition of goddess reverence and respect for women peculiar to Gnosticism, while cropping up everywhere along the historical continuum from the ancient community that left the Nag Hammadi library in Egypt to the Cathars to the theosophists in the nineteenth century.[25]

The truth of the matter is that the Gnostics, not to mention the Cathars, did not necessarily treat women humanely and justly, even though they allowed them privileges the orthodox church with its masculine priesthood denied them. It is more the case that the Gnostics were contemptuous of all hierarchy and moral prohibitions.

Allowing females to engage in "priestly" activity was more an expression of contempt toward the powers that be, not to mention a type of social laissez-faire, than any authentic regard for the well-being of women. Most Gnostics were ethical anarchists.

The same can be said of their elevation of feminine archetypes in their myths and services. The divine feminine in the Gnostic cosmology was often abject and licentious. It was antipatriarchal, but it was not necessarily ennobling.

Historically speaking, the language and imagery of alternative religiosity often becomes bizarre and cultic, especially when it is ruthlessly suppressed, as happened in the West for many centuries. The occult, or secretive, lineage that persists rarely has any historical connection with its initial sources.

The tales of the Templars are a case in point. After their suppression, many admirers began to spin out fantastic accounts of a concealed Templar inheritance that over time came to resemble the very charges that Philip IV and the Inquisition had fabricated about them. The Templars were believed to be powerful magicians, or even satanists, and they were actually venerated for these reasons.[26]

In reality, the medieval Templars were not occultists, although they may have taken more liberties with Christian dogma than would have been prudent in their position. About the worst that could be said of them was that a good number of them did become corrupted. They turned worldly, luxurious, and avaricious, as did many monastics of the age. In that respect, the warrior monks who called themselves the Knights of the Temple of Solomon did not behave much differently.

Whereas a familiar contemporary accusation against Christianity has been that it is inherently patriarchal, the historical record indicates that the opposite may be true. So many of the "evangelical" attempts in the Middle Ages and early modern era to purify the church and guide it back to its apostolic sources were relatively antipatriarchal beneath the skin.

The Sophian Renaissance of the twelfth century that spawned troubadour literature, the valor of the Templars, the cultural sophistication and divine love poetry of the Cistercian monasteries, the Gothic cathedrals, and an affection for the new "queen of heaven" that emerged as a highly cultivated style of Marianism was part and parcel of the legacy of the Christian West. Just as Jesus' own Sophian insurrection had belonged within Judaism, the movement of Western religion since the Middle Ages toward an acceptance of the Two in One can be found at the heart of Christendom.

The story of the divine feminine within Western religious history is not one of multiple voices within the history of religions. Male and female have a common voice, even if only the former has been routinely heard.

And it is to the long-range and concrete implications of that realization to which we must now turn.

5
Toward a Revelation of the Twin-Faced Godhead

I saw the holy city, new Jerusalem, coming down out of heaven from God, made ready like a bride adorned for her husband.—Rev. 21:2

The theological key to discerning what is signified by the divine feminine in history can be found in the book of Revelation.

Because the book of Revelation, or the Apocalypse of John, as it is technically known in the Bible, has been read repeatedly down through the ages as an encrypted prophecy of singular future events, its general import and rhetorical makeup has been given short shrift.

Biblical historicism in the twentieth century, by the same token, has virtually dismissed the possibility that the baffling scenarios in Revelation involving earthly cataclysms, angelic wars in heaven, and the appearance of strange monsters or "beasts" has anything to do with current, or immediate, events. Instead such a historicism has tended to zero in on the social and political upheavals contemporary to the writing of the Apocalypse to which the obscure literary drama might consciously refer.

For example, by this reckoning the "beast" of chapter 13 becomes a code name for the emperor Nero who horribly persecuted Christians during the first century, the fall of Babylon means the eventual doom of the "wicked" city of Rome, and so forth. The scholarly consensus in recent generations has been that Revelation was composed by a Christian martyr and prophet, confined to a "prison camp" on the Greek island of Patmos during the reign of the emperor Domitian.

Furthermore, according to this analysis, the purpose of the book was to offer hope and encouragement to other martyrs of the early church, as Roman authorities killed and tortured many of them who balked at worshiping the statue of the emperor, as required of all citizens by edict from Rome. The refusal of the "saints" to bow down before the "image of the beast" in chapter 13 thus becomes a veiled allusion to this form of protest.

The problem with the historicist argument is that it leaves almost wholly untouched the lush imagery and frightening cosmic spectacle that makes up the Apocalypse. In addition, it does not satisfactorily explain the systematic and precise manner in which so much of Old Testament prophecy is folded and tucked like a valuable linen sheet into the lengthy text of Revelation.

A naive reading of Revelation from the standpoint of literary style and structure makes it abundantly obvious that the anonymous author was more concerned with keeping intact, while embellishing, the core of an apocalyptic legacy than with calling attention to the happenings of his day. The traditional scholarly view that the apocalyptic writers used Old Testament symbols as a code for their still undeciphered communications to each other begs the question.

If the book of Revelation is really nothing more than a cryptogram of the early Christian community, why has it made such a powerful impact on the mind and spirit of all peoples in the West—and not just the pious and devout—for almost two millennia? The early Christians were ultimately interested in proclaiming their gospel, not concealing it. And the fact that this unintelligible writing was readily adopted as part of the Christian canon may say a lot more about its importance for the ancient church than we moderns have cared to admit.

Biblical interpreters, who are apt to shy away from Revelation, can find clues as to what John is really saying by examining the text itself, and by checking cross-references with earlier passages in the Old Testament. Twentieth-century biblical scholarship has been so preoccupied with uncovering the historical circumstances, including the idiosyncrasies of language, under which a text came into existence, it has frequently overlooked the obvious.

It has often neglected to do what anthropologists and linguists dub a structural analysis of the forms and functions of the rhetoric of the text in relation to the whole of the biblical corpus in which it was first located. After doing such a structural analysis, biblical interpretation thus is able to deconstruct the text, which simply means it can show how earlier passages have been deliberately used *to produce a different kind of meaning than was originally intended.*

The biblical writers themselves were always engaged in acts of deconstruction. This method can be seen as part of the interpretative style of the wisdom writers.

For instance, in Luke 7 we have Jesus' explanation of the relationship between his ministry and that of John the Baptist. Jesus tells "the crowds," who were following after the Baptist and had come to see their "prophet" in the flesh, that John

> is the man of whom Scripture says,
> "Here is my herald, whom I send on ahead of you,
> and he will prepare your way before you."
> I tell you, there is not a mother's son greater
> than he. (Luke 7:27–28)

The irony of Jesus' use of the familiar "messianic" saying is conspicuous.

First, by quoting from the Isaianic tradition Jesus seems to suggest that John is intimately connected with the imminent messianic event about to transpire in Galilee. Luke himself says earlier in the Gospel that "the people were on the tiptoe of expectation, all wondering about John, whether perhaps he was the Messiah" (Luke 3:15).

Luke then quotes John as disclaiming any messianic office, as do the other Synoptic authors, who quote the Baptist as deferring to the One whom Christians would later identify as Jesus. "I baptize you with water," John declares to the people, "but there is one to come who is mightier than I" (Luke 3:16).

Yet Jesus employs this same theme initially to refer to John—four chapters after John's own disclaimer—so that a cautious reader, who has not been "hardwired" in the brain to discern automatically Christian dogma, might very well become confused. Rhetorically, Jesus builds John up in the eyes of the people, then deconstructs such a claim by uttering what on the surface sounds like a gross contradiction: "Yet the least in the kingdom of God is greater than [John]" (Luke 7:28).

Several verses later Jesus juxtaposes the popular view that John was a madman with an even stronger suspicion about the "Son of Man." The Son of Man is worse than one, like John, who is "possessed." He is a "glutton and a drinker, a friend of tax-gatherers and sinners!" (Luke 7:34).

But then the following verse provides the clincher to what this jumble of seemingly discontinuous statements, in fact, means: "And yet God's [Sophia] is proved right by all who are her children" (Luke 7:35).

The feminine side of the divine—God's Wisdom, or Sophia—is disclosed as the key to resolving what from the point of view of theological tradition and traditional morality appears as unsolvable contradictions! In the "kingdom" of Sophia—the one, true eschatological kingdom—it does not matter who is the messiah, or the "greatest," or the true "son of God." The eschatological kingdom—the kingdom of Sophia—is the one in which even John, and perhaps the earthly Jesus himself, are among "the least."

In the conventional mind-set Jesus as the eschatological "Son of Man" appears debauched, and consorts with those who have morally stumbled, and fallen. His worldly deportment and his self-designations during the period of his ministry ultimately mean nothing, contrary to what has been written over the centuries in reams of biblical commentary. The very persona and sayings of Jesus are acts of deconstructing, in the style of wisdom, the conventional structure of interpretation and understanding.

Jesus as Messiah brings an "end" to all messianic expectations, particularly those focusing on a divine hero, the "God-man" of the ancient world whose most appropriate incarnation was "the beast" Caesar. As Son of Man and Son of Sophia he comes to vindicate all who are "Sophia's children."

For the Sophia of this passage, as a footnote in the *New English Bible* puts it, "is the personified source of revelation."[1]

In the Solomonic and Isaianic sense "revelation" is always something that is rejected by most of those who hear it. Sophia, the "whore" of the marketplace who "cries aloud in the open air," is scorned and rejected as an almost inevitable prelude to the apocalyptic woes.

Sophia says:

> But because you refused to listen when I called,
> because no one attended when I stretched out my hand,
> because you spurned all my advice
> and would have nothing to do with my reproof,
> I in my turn will laugh at your doom
> and deride you when terror comes upon you,
> when terror comes upon you like a hurricane
> and your doom descends like a whirlwind.
>
> (Prov. 1:24–27)

In the passage from Luke cited above, Jesus alludes to this very line about "Wisdom," or Sophia. "How can I describe the people of this generation?" Jesus asks the crowd. "They are like children sitting in the market-place" (Luke 7:31–32).

Unlike "Sophia's children," the true Israel, they are deaf to the proclamation of the kingdom. The "Pharisees and lawyers," by refusing to be baptized and to hear the good news, have "rejected God's purpose for themselves" (Luke 7:30). In consequence, they will suffer the apocalyptic terrors, as the woman of the marketplace prophesied.

The Codes of Revelation

Returning to Revelation itself, we find that the Apocalypse is not simply the last book of the Bible, but a kind of compendium of codes that run throughout the Old Testament, codes that must be broken so that revelation can take place. In essence, Revelation is a sort of master index for the wisdom tradition. It is a thesaurus of interwoven riddles, prophecies, visions, and veiled sayings that lead to an eschatological summation of the larger tradition of faith from the Christian point of view.

The relationship between Revelation and the Christian Bible itself, therefore, can be understood in a less haphazard way than modern scholarship has allowed. From a literary, if not a theological, standpoint Revelation constitutes the eschatological knotting of the threads of sacred history discerned in the events of the ancient world.

The enormous breadth of cross-textual references in Revelation itself suggests this possibility. But there is another and less obvious way of reading Revelation that goes right to the core of the issue concerning the relationship between the divine masculine and the divine feminine.

As biblical interpreters have often noted, the imagery and vocabulary of Revelation is decidedly influenced by the book of Ezekiel. The book of Ezekiel consists of a series of strange and overpowering visions afforded to a prophet from among the Jews of the sixth century B.C.E. deported by Nebuchadnezzar to Babylon.

In that respect, the historical and editorial contexts of both Ezekiel and Revelation are quite similar. John, a likely prisoner of imperial Rome, was captive on the island of Patmos in the Aegean Sea when he had his experiences. Ezekiel was "among the exiles by the river Kebar." Like John, Ezekiel declares, "The heavens were opened and I saw a vision of God" (Ezek. 1:1).

Other parallels are telling as well. The content of the visions that are supposed to have occurred in the sixth century B.C.E. and the first century C.E. remains largely the same. Both seers behold "living creatures" that have a human form (Ezek. 1:28; Rev. 4:6–8). Both hear what sounds like the roar of rushing waters (Ezek. 1:24; Rev. 1:15). Both see a figure who seems to be like brass glowing in a fire (Ezek. 1:27; Rev. 1:15). Both experience the unrolling of a scroll, which they are commanded to eat (Ezek. 2:9–3:3; Rev. 10:8–10). Both are preoccupied in some manner with the city of Jerusalem and its fate.

There are some interesting divergences, however. John in the book of Revelation has a vision of "one like a son of man" (Rev. 1:13). Ezekiel himself is addressed as "son of man."

The last nine chapters of Ezekiel (Ezekiel 40–48), which some commentators believe amount to a later addition, expound at length on the layout of a "new Jerusalem" at which the prophet gazes from a high mountain. At the end of Revelation, John too is taken to a high mountain, where he looks on a holy "city" portrayed in much the same language and with some of the precise architectural detail as Ezekiel's (Rev. 21:10–22:5).

Yet, while Ezekiel dwells on a description of the temple in the new city, the author of Revelation avows flatly, "I saw no temple in the city; for its temple was the sovereign LORD God and the Lamb" (Rev. 21:22).

While it is plain that Ezekiel's "new Jerusalem" is an actual site for human habitation, drawn up according to the specifications of the ancient priestly theocracy, John's is a cipher.

Because of the location within the text itself of Ezekiel's vision, not to mention its appearance after the catastrophic destruction of the historical Temple at Jerusalem, we can reasonably deduce that these Old Testament passages may have been a blueprint for the rebuilding of Solomon's great edifice after the return of the Jews to Palestine during the reign of the Persian king Cyrus around 500 B.C.E. The building plans themselves were "revealed" from on high. Thus the sanctity of the temple during Hellenistic, and Roman, times may have been secured by this priestly use of the recorded oracles of an earlier prophet.

The seer known as John, on the other hand, has no interest in reviving the agenda of the Davidic theocracy whose authority had already been destroyed, or was about to be destroyed, by Roman legions, depending on when one dates the book of Revelation.[2] The restoration of a priestly theocracy, for which Ezekiel and perhaps his successors may have hoped, is the farthest thing from John's mind. John paraphrases the ancient theocratic text only to deconstruct and hence deconsecrate it.

Indeed, what is most intriguing about John's reworking of this traditional Jewish material is his clear identification of Ezekiel's "new Jerusalem" with "the bride, the wife of the Lamb" (Rev. 21:9).

This particular passage in Revelation has always flustered biblical exegetes. The new Jerusalem is not described as an actual city, but as a beautiful woman who is prepared for "marriage" to the Lamb of God, which orthodox Christianity has taken as the name for Christ. From Paul onward, the "bride" was understood as a metaphor for the church itself. The marriage to the Lamb signified the covenantal relationship between the Christian believers and the risen Jesus.

However, consideration of the actual structure of Revelation prompts the conclusion that something more is afoot. Just as John, at the climax of the very entire eschatological drama, carefully and forcefully deconstructs the temple mythology of the Davidic priesthood, so he introduces a motif that would have been unthinkable to classic Judaism—a "sacred marriage" (Rev. 19:6–9).

Sacred marriages were quite common among the heathen practices of the ancient Near East, and constituted one of the central practices that the Deuteronomic writers of the Old Testament inveighed against.

Sacred marriages involved sexual intercourse between a king and his consort, who was frequently a temple harlot. The purpose of the sacred marriage, from a ritual standpoint, was to unite the energies of male and female "divinity" in ensuring the fertility of the countryside.

The wedding and "wedding-supper" of the bride and Lamb, however, have a different significance in Revelation. The sacred marriage of Revelation is contrasted with the "fornications" that human beings have committed with another woman, the "great whore" known as Babylon, whose perfidy and doom is described in Revelation 14–18.

Both the new Jerusalem and Babylon are concurrently characterized as "cities." In archaic mythology cities were sometimes viewed as embodiments of goddesses, with which commerce was a form of "sexual" engagement. The so-called whore of Babylon is also "the great city that holds sway over the kings of the earth" (Rev. 17:18) and with whom they have committed "fornication" (Rev. 17:2).

It is easy to read "Babylon" as Rome in the historical context. Indeed, the ferocity with which John condemns the "great whore" might be expected of one who, along with his comrades, had suffered torments at the hands of her imperial administration.

Yet there is something basically wrong with this familiar interpretation.

First, we have this suggestive passage in Revelation 17, where the angel speaking to John explains his vision:

> Then he said to me, "The ocean you saw, where the great whore sat, is an ocean of peoples and populations, nations and languages. As for the ten horns you saw, they together with the beast will come to hate the whore; they will strip her naked and leave her desolate; they will batten on her flesh and burn her to ashes. For God has put it into their heads to carry out his purpose, by making common cause and conferring their sovereignty upon the beast until all that God has spoken is fulfilled." (Rev. 17:15–17)

The vision of Babylon's sudden devastation does not correspond to any historic reality, particularly if the "name" that John says has a "secret meaning" (Rev. 17:4) were indeed to be "Rome." Rome "fell" only four centuries after the writing of Revelation, and it did not fall in a "day."

In addition, the same cheap historicism that identifies the "beast" as Caesar and the "whore" as Rome takes little account of the passage cited above in which the beast, allied with the other "horns," makes war on the harlot in order to carry through with God's "purpose."

In the apocalyptic tradition the horns are usually associated with historical empires. So the conspiracy of the beast and the horns would more likely correspond to the various imperial regimes, including that of Rome, who had occupied Palestine since the destruction of the first Temple.

In this context it is evident that the whore must signify the city of Jerusalem itself, which had recently been stripped naked and burned to ashes. In keeping with the symmetry of the concluding chapters of Revelation, the whore with whom many "fornicate" is theocratic and androcentric Judaism. The "bride" is the new, eschatological reality embodied in the followers of Sophia—whom the Romans derisively referred to as Christians.

It is possible to construe the "bride" herself as Sophia. John's eschatological "sacred marriage" would be the cosmic version of the "spiritual" union performed by the Therapeutae in the desert communities.

Furthermore, there are indications that John was preoccupied with the issue of Sophian eschatology.

Beginning with Revelation 2, we have the so-called addresses to the seven churches in Asia Minor. Each address begins with the phrase "These are the words of." Each of these phrases seeks to ground the authority of the divine voice that is speaking.

Christian orthodoxy has assumed that the "voice" speaking to the seven churches is that of Jesus. But the author of Revelation is rather coy about the voice behind the vision itself. For example, the opening of the Apocalypse of John declares boldly, "This is the revelation given by God *to* Jesus Christ" (Rev. 1:1, italics added). In other words, Revelation has something to do with the totality of the Christian "mysteries" themselves, of which Jesus is primarily the hierophant, the one who unveils them. He is not the sole and exclusive embodiment of everything that was and would be revealed to the human race, as orthodoxy has long maintained.

Moreover, it is apparent from the context that the divine figure in the first chapter, who appears to John from the heavenly realms, is neither the historical Jesus nor precisely the Jesus of the Apostles' Creed. He is alternately described as "one like a son of man," as an "angel," as "the first and the last." But he is never named as Jesus in the familiar, canonical sense. Indeed, the messianic figure who comes riding on a white horse with the "opening of heaven" at the moment of the final, apocalyptic battle in Revelation 19 has "a name known to none but himself" (Rev. 19:12).

In each of the addresses to the seven churches, however, the identity of the voice from which the revelation to John emanates successively unfolds. The "words" are those of "the One who holds the seven stars in his right hand" (Rev. 2:1), of "the First and the Last" (Rev. 2:8), of the "One who has the sharp two-edged sword" (Rev. 2:12), of the "Son of God" (Rev. 2:18), of "the One who holds the seven spirits of God, the seven stars" (Rev. 3:1), of "the holy one, the true one, who holds the key of David" (Rev. 3:7), of "the Amen, the faithful and true witness, the prime source of all God's creation" (Rev. 3:14).

At times the voice itself speaks in the first person. The voice declares at the beginning, "I am the Alpha and the Omega . . . who is and who was and who is to come, the sovereign LORD of all" (Rev. 1:8), and at the end, "Behold! I am making all things new! . . . I am the Alpha and the Omega" (Rev. 21:5–6).

At the very end of Revelation a first-person speaker does refer to himself finally as Jesus.[3] But it remains murky whether the Jesus speaking here who bears the "testimony" or revelation "given" to him by God coincides precisely with the source of the other voices. The voices themselves in Revelation seem to override each other and fuse in a kind of a capella harmony. The question remains, though: Who is the voice that calls itself "the Alpha and the Omega"?

The phrase "Alpha and Omega," of course is used exclusively throughout the Bible for the transcendent Godhead, the "sovereign Lord of all." And it is in this connection that the question of the engendering Godhead looms very large.

There is no doubt that the voice of ultimate reality in Revelation is of the male gender. According to the grammar of the text, the voice is regularly designated as "he." But can it be female as well? The voice of the Godhead also sounds very much like Sophia.

The statement in Revelation 21:5 ("Behold! I am making all things new!") is one of only two snippets of text in Revelation where, according to a footnote in the *New English Bible,* God directly speaks.[4] The cross-reference to "making all things new" is usually given as Isaiah 43:19, but that particular Old Testament passage has a far more limited significance.

The meaning in Isaiah concerns the appearance of Yahweh in all his eschatological glory. The accent falls on the manifestation in full splendor of the Holy One of Israel and the adoration of him during the restoration of the fortunes of his chosen people.[5]

The aforementioned lines of Revelation, however, speak of total world transformation, *the making anew of the whole creation.* Interestingly, that job, according to the Wisdom of Solomon, is reserved for Sophia. "She is but one, yet can do everything; herself unchanging, she makes all things new" (Wisd. Sol. 7:27).

Furthermore, the "one like a son of man" who holds the "seven stars" alludes to the royal iconography of Sophian eschatological kingship. Sophia, as the Wisdom of Solomon says, is "more radiant than the sun and surpasses every constellation" (Wisd. Sol. 7:29). She is responsible for the rise and fall of empires. She is the throne behind all thrones (Wisd. Sol. 6:20–21).

Although the mythological correlate in the ancient world to the vision of the "seven stars" held by the Son of Man remains uncertain, it was apparently an emblem of the Caesars themselves, as Roman coins show. But it may also be associated with the seven stars visible in the summer sky of the northern hemisphere, and known as the Pleiades, or "seven sisters."

In classical lore the Pleiades were closely connected with the divine feminine in its "queenly" aspects. In Greek religion the Pleiades themselves were the half-sisters of the Hyades, who nursed the divine "lord" Dionysus, the pagan mythic correlate of the "suffering savior."

Thus the disclosure that the Son of Man, or Son of Sophia, holds the Pleiades in his hands may tell us something very important about what was at stake in the book of Revelation. The early Christian community was confronted with the rising cult of Caesar worship, which may have appropriated the symbolism of the Dionysiac folklore of Asia Minor.

As the Son of Sophia, the real "Son of God," the "true one, who holds the key of David," the community claimed the eschatological Lordship of Jesus on the basis of something more profound, and more compelling to the Gentile world, than the lineage of an ancient Jewish king.

As the spouse of Wisdom, Jesus became the male, imperial counterpart to the "Great Goddess." The early Christians maintained that only their risen Christ, more powerful than either Caesar or Dionysus, could be addressed as "Lord."

The Two in One

But that may be pushing the actual text of Revelation beyond its syntactical limits. What matters in this case is that Revelation points toward an encounter with the full meaning of the Bible itself, which is the unveiling of the twin-faced Godhead—the Two in One.

The book of Revelation resounds with the veritable voice of the Two in One. The last lines of Revelation, like the powerful and dramatic concluding notes of a Beethoven symphony, manifest this dyadic voice.

The last lines contain the so-called maranatha, the invocation using an obscure Aramaic phrase of the final "coming"—*parousia* in Greek—

of God in fullness, as an unconcealed "total presence." " 'Come!' say the Spirit and the bride. 'Come!' let each hearer reply. Come forward, you who are thirsty; accept the water of life, a free gift to all who desire it" (Rev. 22:17). And, later, "Come, LORD Jesus!" (Rev. 22:20).

The voice of invocation is that of "the Spirit and the bride." What does that signify? The Spirit and the Bride signify the "sacred marriage" in the highest sense of the word. That is the "coming" toward which the Bible, from the Christian standpoint at least, points.

It is the "coming" that should also be understood as the eschatological direction of current faith. It is the *coming together of man and woman* in the celebration of the Two in One, in a parousia through which the ancient symbols of the faith at last become intelligible, and powerful in a new manner of speaking. For all faith is constituted in the shadow of the eschaton, in anticipation of the presence in which God fully "dwells with human beings," as Revelation puts it, when "the old order has passed away" (Rev. 21:4). The old order is patriarchal Judaism and Christianity. But the "new heaven and earth" that constitute God's order of things still remains "not quite yet," even though in the divine sense "they are already fulfilled" (Rev. 21:5).

As we approach the millennium we must listen closely to the antiphonal voice of the sovereign LORD of history who becomes incarnate as male and female, as the Two in One.

The absence of a temple in the holy city signifies that, as Jesus' own eschatological discourses in Matthew 24 concerning the destruction of the Temple at Jerusalem portend, the new temple is that of the human body. And the human body is gendered. It is a city both divided and united in the mystery of male and female.

The practical implications of the theological idea of the Two in One are absolutely enormous.

First, the current split between traditionalists and feminists in the reading of scripture can be overcome. Both sides are harking to the voice of the Alpha and the Omega. Both sides can claim to have experienced a limited dimension of the limitless Godhead.

Second, the task of gender relationships under the aspect of eternity can be seen as the task of making faith itself concrete, of putting into practice the engendering Gospel. The estrangement between man and woman that has so characterized the twentieth century reflects a sense of estrangement in our relationship to the divine itself.

For one sex to deny, to abuse, or to subjugate the other is to dishonor God. For one sex to claim preeminence over the other is to commit the most abominable form of idolatry. For one sex to believe it can live fully without the other is to reject the very fullness of the holy.

Third, the wrongheaded assumption that in order to recapture the sense of the divine feminine and exalt it as equal to the divine masculine one must reject the Western religious tradition now must be cast aside. The record of religious revolutions is always one of rereading texts.

We must now reread the tradition and its scriptural foundations in ways that we have never read them before. We must now think theologically about scripture and tradition in a manner that has hitherto remained unthought.

We must now await the coming of the beginning of a new thousand-year cycle of years with a joy and anticipation that may never have been experienced since those early days in Jerusalem, now almost two millennia ago.

We must pray, and say, *maranatha* in an entirely new way. We must say, "I see Thee in you, and you in me."

We must say, "Our sovereign LORD, Alpha and Omega, the Two in One—come!"

Notes

1: The Engendering Godhead

1. Some writers have challenged the notion that the God of the Old Testament can be considered both male and female, noting that such a deity creates and is involved with the world in an asexual way, as contrasted with the prevalence of actual sexual intercourse in the cosmologies throughout the ancient Near East. This argument is made rather forcefully by Judith Ochshorn in *The Female Experience and the Nature of the Divine* (Bloomington, Ind.: Indiana University Press, 1981), 139ff. Ochshorn, however, assumes that the experience of divine gender must be tied closely with sacred sexuality, which is not necessarily the case.

2. See René Girard, *Violence and the Sacred* (New Haven, Conn.: Yale University Press, 1978).

3. See Elaine Pagels, *The Gnostic Gospels* (New York: Random House, 1979).

4. Some scholars have even postulated an Iranian influence on the development of the Jewish idea of Wisdom. The idea is that the Jews received the Iranian myth at the time they were captive in Babylon. The Babylonians, in turn, had taken it from the Persians. See O. S. Rankin, *Israel's Wisdom Literature* (New York: Schocken Books, 1969), 252ff.

5. Georg Fohrer, "Sophia," in James L. Crenshaw, ed., *Studies in Ancient Israelite Wisdom* (New York: KTAV Publishing House, 1976), 63–83.

6. Johann Wolfgang von Goethe, *Faust: Part One & Part Two,* trans. Charles E. Passage (New York: Bobbs-Merrill, Co., 1965), 15.

2: Old Testament and Other Ancient Sources

1. Klaas A. D. Smelik, *Writings from Ancient Israel: A Handbook of Historical and Religious Documents,* trans. G. I. Davies (Louisville, Ky.: Westminster/John Knox Press, 1992), 5.

2. Raphael Patai, *The Hebrew Goddess* (New York: KTAV Publishing House, 1967), 20–21. Patai's thesis is argued and discussed at length in Anne Baring and Jules Cashford, *The Myth of the Goddess: Evolution of an Image* (New York: Viking Arkana, 1991), 447–78. See also Raphael Patai, "The Goddess Cult in the Hebrew-Jewish Religion," in Agehananda Bharati, ed., *The Realm of the Extra-Human: Agents and Audiences* (The Hague: Mouton Publishers, 1976). Patai's thesis, of course, remains rather controversial among scholars and is still considered speculative. Other articles that treat the subject in a different way are Edward Lipinski, "The Goddess Atirat in Ancient Arabia," *Orientalia lovaniensia Periodica* 3 (1972): 101–19; David West, "The Semitic Origins of Ariadne and Atalanta," *Ugarit-Forschungen* 22 (1991): 425–32; Helgard Balz-Chochois, "Gomer oder die Macht der Astarte," *Evangelische Theologie* 42 (Jan.–Feb. 1982): 37–65.

3. Patai, *Hebrew Goddess*, 29.

4. For a discussion of the Queen of Heaven theme, see Susan Ackerman, " 'And the Women Knead Dough': The Worship of the Queen of Heaven in Sixth-Century Judah," in Peggy L. Day, ed., *Gender and Difference in Ancient Israel* (Philadelphia: Fortress Press, 1989), 109–24.

5. See Jer. 44:15–28. As Walter Rast observes, the women "give voice to what must have been a prevalent view of the time, that the goddess, whether Ishtar in Mesopotamia or Astarte in Palestine, possessed a unique capacity to ensure protection and prosperity. On the other hand, no discernible way out of the terrors of the moment seemed to be present in the silence and apparent inactivity of Yahweh. The tradition describes the prophet as hard put to say it just the opposite way. According to him their activities were not the way toward a better future, but a desperate act leading to waste and desolation." "Cakes for the Queen of Heaven," in Arthur L. Merrill and Thomas W. Overholt, eds., *Scripture in History and Theology: Essays in Honor of J. Coert Rylaarsdam* (Pittsburgh: Pickwick Press, 1977), 175–76.

6. Patai, *Hebrew Goddess*, 271.

7. Baring and Cashford, *Myth of the Goddess*, 476–77.

8. See Glendon E. Bryce, *A Legacy of Wisdom: The Egyptian Contribution to the Wisdom of Israel* (Lewisburg, Pa.: Bucknell University Press, 1979).

9. Philo, *Proverbs 8:22.*

10. See Patai, *Hebrew Goddess*, 142f.

11. See Matt. 26:59–62: "The chief priests and the whole Council tried to find some allegation against Jesus on which a death-sentence could be based; but they failed to find one, though many came forward with false evidence. Finally two men alleged that he had said, 'I can pull down the temple of God, and rebuild it in three days.' At this the High Priest rose and said to him, 'Have you no answer to the charge that these witnesses bring against you?'"

12. See Luke 19:35b–38: "Then they threw their cloaks on the colt, for Jesus to mount, and they carpeted the road with them as he went on

his way. And now, as he approached the descent from the Mount of Olives, the whole company of his disciples in their joy began to sing aloud the praises of God for all the great things they had seen:

> 'Blessings on him who comes as king in the name of the LORD!
> Peace in heaven, glory in highest heaven!'

13. See note to Luke 19:38, *The New English Bible* (New York: Oxford University Press, 1972), 98.

14. J. Gwyn Griffiths, "The Great Egyptian Cults of Oecumenical Spiritual Significance," in A. H. Armstrong, ed., *Classical Mediterranean Spirituality* (New York: Crossroad, 1986), 47.

15. For discussions of Isis in this capacity, see C. J. Bleeker, "Isis as Saviour Goddess" in S.G.F. Brandon, ed., *The Saviour God: Comparative Studies in the Concept of Salvation* (New York: Barnes & Noble, 1963), 1–15; Frederick W. Norris, "Isis, Sarapis and Demeter in Antioch of Syria," *Harvard Theological Review* 75:2 (1982):189–207; Gail Paterson Corrington, "The Milk of Salvation: Redemption by the Mother in Late Antiquity and Early Christianity," *Harvard Theological Review* 82:4 (1989): 393–420; R. E. Witt, "Some Thoughts on Isis in Relation to Mithras," in John R. Hinnels, ed., *Mithraic Studies*, vol. 2 (Manchester: Manchester University Press, 1971), 479–93.

16. Howard Clark Kee, "Myth and Miracle: Isis, Wisdom, and the Logos of John," in Alan M. Olson, ed., *Myth, Symbol, and Reality* (Notre Dame, Ind.: University of Notre Dame Press, 1980), 145.

17. See Rory B. Egan, "Isis: Goddess of the Oikoumene," in Larry W. Hurtado, ed., *Goddesses in Religion and Modern Debate* (Atlanta: Scholars Press, 1990), 128ff.

18. Ibid., 140.

3: From Eleusis to Early Christianity

1. For the most recent appraisals of the Eleusian mysteries, see Ken Dowden, "Grades in the Eleusian Mysteries, "*Revue de l'histoire des religions* 197 (Oct.–Dec. 1980): 409–27; Nita Ludwig, "The Christian Mythos: Christianity and the History of Ritual and Initiation," *Epiphany* 2 (1982): 28–39; Luther H. Martin, "Those Elusive Eleusinian Mystery Shows," *Society of Biblical Literature 1984 Seminar Papers* (Chico, Calif.: Scholars Press, 1984), 264–68; Christine Downing, "Persephone in Hades," *Anima* 4 (1977): 22–29.

2. Plato characterizes philosophy, for example, as a form of "initiation" and philosophical knowledge a kind of "mystery." See *Phaedrus*. Both the *Phaedrus* and the *Phaedo* can be read as coded reinscriptions of the Eleusian experience, where the soul ascends out of darkness to a direct encounter with the shining *eidoi*, "forms"—in effect, a divine vision granting immortality, which was the fulfillment of the mysteries.

3. Apuleius, *The Golden Ass,* trans. Jack Lindsay (Bloomington, Ind.: Indiana University Press, 1962), 235–36.

4. Ibid., 237–38.

5. See Walter Burkert, *Ancient Mystery Cults* (Cambridge, Mass.: Harvard University Press, 1987), 21.

6. See G.R.H. Wright, "The Mother-Maid at Bethlehem," in *Zeitschrift für die altestamentliche Wissenchaft* (Berlin and New York: Walter de Gruyter, 1986), 56–72. See also Walter Burkert, *Structure and History in Greek Mythology and Ritual* (Berkeley, Calif.: University of California Press, 1979), esp. chap. 6.

7. The name "De-meter" is now generally regarded by scholars as meaning "barley-mother," even though the cultivation of barley was predominant in the Levant. According to Wright, the similarity of the names may suggest a common origin of the two cults.

8. Wright, "Mother-Maid at Bethlehem," 68.

9. See John S. Kloppenborg, "Isis and Sophia in the Book of Wisdom," *Harvard Theological Review* 75:1 (1982): 57–84.

10. See Samuel Sandmel, gen. ed., *The New English Bible,* Apocrypha (New York: Oxford University Press, 1972), 97n1.

11. See Richard Horsley, "Spiritual Marriage with Sophia," *Vigiliae christianae* 33:48. A survey of the literature that shows the identification of "Lady Wisdom" with Christ can be found in Rebecca D. Pentz, "Jesus as Sophia," *The Reformed Journal* 38 (1988): 17–22. See also John Ashton, "The Transformation of Wisdom: A Study of the Prologue of John's Gospel," *New Testament Studies* 32 (1986): 161–86.

12. Elisabeth Schüssler Fiorenza, *In Memory of Her: A Feminist Theological Reconstruction of Christian Origins* (New York: Crossroad, 1983), 213.

13. See James M. Robinson, "Jesus as Sophos and Sophia: Wisdom Tradition and the Gospels," in Robert L. Wilken, ed., *Aspects of Wisdom in Judaism and Early Christianity* (Notre Dame, Ind.: University of Notre Dame Press, 1975), 5. See also Luke 7:33–35.

14. See Anne Baring and Jules Cashford, *The Myth of the Goddess: Evolution of an Image* (New York: Viking Arkana, 1991), 620.

15. See, for example, 1 Cor. 1:24: "To those who have heard his call, Jews and Greeks alike, he is the power of God and the [Sophia] of God." Here the figure found in Proverbs of "Wisdom" who calls, who is feminine in the Old Testament, is transformed into the masculine Jesus. Other metamorphoses of the female Sophia into the masculine Jesus, Christ, or "Word of God" can be found in John 1:1–14; Eph. 3:9; Col. 1:15–20.

16. Elisabeth Schüssler Fiorenza, "Wisdom Mythology and the Christological Hymns of the New Testament," in Wilken, *Aspects of Wisdom,* 34.

17. Rose Horman Arthur, "The Wisdom Goddess and the Masculinization of Western Religion," in Ursula King, ed., *Women in the World's Religions: Past and Present* (New York: Paragon House, 1987), 25.

18. See Horsley, "Spiritual Marriage with Sophia," 35. Also J. Paschke, *He Basilike Hodos* (Paderoborn, 1931) 9f:262–64.

19. Similarities between portrayals of Isis and the Jewish figure of Sophia are sketched by Hans Conzelmann. See *Die Mutter der Weisheit in Zeit und Geschichte* (New York: Viking Arkana, 1991), 609.

20. Quoted in Horsley, "Spiritual Marriage with Sophia," 35.

21. For a discussion of this problem, see Rose Horman Arthur, *The Wisdom Goddess: Feminine Motifs in Eight Nag Hammadi Documents* (Lanham, Md.: University Press of America, 1984).

22. See Horsley, "Spiritual Marriage with Sophia," 49.

23. See R. Alan Culpepper, *The Johannine School: An Evaluation of the Johannine-School Hypothesis Based on an Investigation of the Nature of Ancient Schools* (Missoula, Mont.: Scholars Press, 1975), 203.

24. Baring and Cashford, *Myth of the Goddess*, 613.

25. Caitlín Matthews, *Sophia Goddess of Wisdom: The Divine Feminine from Black Goddess to World-Soul* (New York: HarperCollins, 1991), 103.

26. See James Muilenburg, "The Son of Man in Daniel and the Ethiopic Apocalypse of Enoch," *Journal of Biblical Literature* 79 (1960): 197–209.

27. See Deidre J. Good, *Reconstructing the Tradition of Sophia in Gnostic Literature* (Atlanta: Scholars Press, 1987), 35.

28. Muilenburg, "Son of Man in Daniel," 208. See also James D. G. Dunn, *Christology in the Making: A New Testament Inquiry into the Origins of the Doctrine of the Incarnation* (Philadelphia: Westminster Press, 1980), 73.

29. Susan Cady, Marian Ronan, Hal Taussig, *Wisdom's Feast: Sophia in Study and Celebration* (New York: Harper & Row, 1986), 38. For a study of how the Jewish Shekinah, the rabbinic form of the Sophia concept who also "dwells" with her people, plays out in John, see John Bowman, *The Fourth Gospel and the Jews: A Study in R. Akiba, Esther, and the Gospel of John* (Pittsburgh: Pickwick Press, 1975), 52ff.

30. Cady et al., *Wisdom's Feast*, 28.

31. Julius Grill, *Untersuchungen über die Entstehung des vierten Evangeliums* (Tübingen: J.C.B. Mohr, 1902), I, 202.

32. Karl-Gustav Sandelin, *Wisdom as Nourisher: A Study of an Old Testament Theme, Its Development within Early Judaism and Its Impact on Early Christianity* (Åbo: Åbo Akademi, 1986), 180.

33. See Felix Christ, *Jesus Sophia: Die Sophia Christologie bei den Synoptikern* (Zurich: Zwingli Verlag, 1970). The main Sophia sayings, according to Christ: Matt. 11:16–19 (cf. Luke 7:31–35); Matt. 23:34–36 (cf. Luke 11:49–51); Luke 10:21; Matt. 23:37–39 (cf. Luke 13:34).

34. Ronald Piper, *Wisdom in the Q-tradition: The Aphoristic Teaching of Jesus* (Cambridge: Cambridge University Press, 1989), 180.

35. Evidence for the claim that a special tradition outside the public forms of Judaism, which centered on the messianic notion of the Son of Man and actually saw the crucifixion as a long-awaited enactment of that figure's divine role, has been developed by Wilhelm Bousset. According

to Bousset, the portraiture of Christ in the Gospel of John may have been an effort to fit the historical facts of Jesus' life, particularly his suffering on the cross, within this hidden messianic tradition. Bousset says the Fourth Gospel shows how "we have before us a clearly recognizable and fixed structure of ideas which for a considerable time played a dominant role in Christian dogmatics." *Kyrios Christos,* trans. John E. Steely (Nashville: Abingdon Press, 1970), 53. The Son of Man, as opposed to the Son of David, was not so much the great monarch as the humble shepherd who, following the bidding of Sophia, went forth into the world to find the missing sheep. This view is corroborated in various sayings of Jesus about the homelessness and destitution of the Son of Man, who adopts the life of those whom he is seeking. His role as messianic redeemer is not in glory, but in self-sacrifice, which leads to true heavenly, as opposed to earthly, exaltation. "The Son of Man came to save the lost" (Matt. 18:11, marg.). See Bousset, 37.

36. An interesting piece of data suggesting that the apocalyptic Son of Man may be related to the very mythic complex out of which the Sophia tradition was born is found in the Fourth Book of Ezra. Ezra has a vision and sees "one like the figure of a man," the common designation for the Son of Man, rise out of the sea (IV Ezra 13:3). In Apuleius's vision Isis rises out of the sea, and the ancient association of Sophia with the Spirit that moved in the beginning on the primeval waters is striking. See Bousset, *Kyrios Christos,* 45. In the studies of ancient mythology by Robert Graves, Aphrodite is "the wise one of the sea," who is also the Holy Spirit who moves on the face of the waters. See Robert Graves, *The White Goddess: A Historical Grammar of Poetic Myth* (New York: Creative Age Press, 1948), 131.

37. See Kloppenborg, "Isis and Sophia," 74.

38. See *The New English Bible,* New Testament, 31.

39. Another passage to enforce this theme that Jesus' self-understanding was different from that of a Davidic messiah can be found in John 1:43–51. The writer of John is more up-front from the outset about who Jesus is, and who he proclaims himself to be, than the authors of the Synoptics. The passage tells of the disciple Philip, who makes a visit to a man named Nathanael, and says, "We have met the man spoken of by Moses in the Law, and by the prophets: it is Jesus son of Joseph, from Nazareth." Nathanael registers surprise and says he cannot believe "anything good come[s] from Nazareth," indicating there is some discrepancy between Jesus' social origins and what is believed about him. When Nathanael finally meets Jesus, he says, "Rabbi, you are the Son of God; you are king of Israel." The suggestion is *that* is how one would expect to address a messianic figure. But Jesus is not flattered and criticizes Nathanael for not getting it, so to speak. Nathanael responds enthusiastically because Jesus has seen him under a "fig-tree"—a messianic allusion in the Davidic tradition and recognized him as a genuine "Israel." But Jesus adds: "Is this the ground of your faith, that I told you I saw you

under the fig-tree? You shall see greater things than that." Then he added, "In truth, in very truth I tell you all, you shall see heaven wide open, and God's angels ascending and descending upon the Son of Man." The "opening of heaven" is the disclosure of the great things of God hidden to the eyes through the ages.

40. *The New English Bible*, New Testament, 98.

41. Another important piece in this jigsaw puzzle may be the mysterious prophecy Isaiah makes in his confrontation with Ahaz, ruler of the Southern Kingdom of Judah, during the time of the Assyrian invasion in the eighth century B.C.E. (Isa. 7:1–8:15). These lines from the dawn of the Christian era were regarded as the key prophecy in the Old Testament of Jesus' coming, but modern historical criticism of the passages has obscured why the early followers of Jesus considered them so important.

On the surface the prophecy—"A young woman is with child, and she will bear a son, and will call him Immanuel" (Isa. 7:14)—can be read as having nothing to do with any grand, future messianic appearance. The simple, historicist interpretation on which most scholars agree is one that makes sense in terms of the events of the time. In 735 B.C.E. Assyria attacked the nations in the western part of Palestine, inciting the king of Israel, the northern realm, and Syria to make an alliance to roll back the invasion. When Ahaz refused to join the coalition, the two neighbors besieged Jerusalem. Ahaz, primarily out of fear of Assyria, decided to ask that ruthless power for assistance against the invaders, whereupon the prophet Isaiah warned the king of Judah not to become entangled in such dangerous liaisons, but to call on Yahweh for help. His counsel to the king was the same as that of the prophets had been from the time of David, "Have firm faith, or you will not stand firm" (Isa. 7:9).

When Ahaz refused to turn to Yahweh and refused to ask a "sign" from the Lord for encouragement, Isaiah uttered the famous prophecy and gave him the "sign" which he had refused—the birth of the child. It is apparent from succeeding verses that the "child" is that of a "prophetess," with whom Isaiah "lay" (Isa. 8:1–4). It was very common for Israelite prophets, and it was also a hallmark of Isaiah's own career, to offer such signs to reinforce their oracular predictions. So why should this passage—aside from the fact that a later literalist without historical sensitivity could indeed be captivated by the simple prophecy of the birth of a child—be considered the key to God's salvation history?

One should note that Isaiah's prophecy in this context is not so much against Ahaz as against "the house of David" (Isa. 7:13). Isaiah asserts flatly that the house of David has worn out "the patience of God." It is because of the lack of faith on the part of the Davidic line of kings as a whole, not just Ahaz, that the child will be born. And the coming of the child will be accompanied by a ruinous decline in the fortunes of the Davidic dynasty. Isaiah prophesies to Ahaz: "[Yahweh] will bring on you, your people, and your house, a time the like of which has not been seen since Ephraim broke away from Judah" (Isa. 7:17). The prophecy anti-cipates the destruction of the nation and the fall of Jerusalem over a cen-tury later. Even though Isaiah could have had in mind the coming As-syrian siege against Jerusalem, which turned out to be a failure that Isaiah himself attributed to the agency of God, it is probable that later tradition saw the prophecy as referring to the wars of Nebuchadnezzar.

In essence, it is easy to surmise that postexilic Judaism looked on the prophecy as that of the downfall of the Davidic monarchy for reasons quite different from those the Deuteronomic writers believed were the cause of God's wrath. The Deuteronomists held that national calamity came in the wake of "whoring after" foreign gods. Isaiah makes it a sim-ple case of an ultimate failure to heed the cryptic and most difficult to discern word of the mysterious Lord of history in a very difficult situa-tion. Ahaz appears to have been relatively clean so far as the evil of idol-atry was concerned. All the sins of the Davidic kings were trivial com-pared to this misstep, which was ultimately fatal for the nation.

The crux of the matter, as we learn in Isa. 8:11–15, is whether Israel is taking the easy way out of a hard situation created by a "hard" God. The theme of a righteous king as taking the hard way, as opposed to the easy chosen by Ahaz, is replayed in the parable of Jesus.

"These were the words of the LORD to me," says Isaiah, "for his hand was strong upon me; and he warned me not to follow the ways of this peo-ple: You shall not say 'too hard' of everything that this people calls hard; you shall neither dread nor fear that which they fear. It is the LORD of Hosts whom you must count 'hard'; he it is whom you must fear and dread. He shall become your 'hardship,' a boulder and a rock which the two houses of Israel shall run against and over which they shall stumble, a trap and a snare to those who live in Jerusalem; and many shall stum-ble over them, many shall fall and be broken, many shall be snared and caught."

The writings of Isaiah, including the pseudo-Isaiah of chapter 40 on-ward, were of course at the center of Christian interpretation of the Old Testament. Biblical scholarship has also identified Isaiah closely with the wisdom tradition. (See Johannes Fichtner, "Isaiah among the Wise," in James L. Crenshaw, ed., *Studies in Ancient Israelite Wisdom*, 429–38; New York: KTAV Publishing House, 1976.) Hence one must wonder: if the Isaianic prophecies were so important, was it not simply because of their messianic content, which can be found in other portions of the Old Tes-tament, or their lofty and poetic diction, which is just as pronounced in the book of Jeremiah, but because of the deeper suggestion about who the successors to the kingship of Israel might actually be? If the Davidic line in the view of this tradition had been cut off deliberately by God be-cause of its faithlessness, was there another hidden, or rejected, dynastic family that could claim the ancient messianic title?

And would not it make sense that such a family, while claiming de-scent from David as we find in the genealogy of Matthew, might see itself more precisely as the heirs of Solomon and the tradition of wisdom? Might such a family, having lived in Egypt and absorbed its cosmopolitan culture, been less nationalistic in its messianic outlook and more universalistic? Might such a family, as outcasts in a country ruled by claimants to the Davidic line from the time of the Maccabees onward, have gone out into the desert in anticipation of the new eschatological kingdom that would be ushered in by a messiah from their own stock at God's chosen moment? Might the implicit social connections between the families of Jesus and John the Baptist hinted at in the opening chapters of the Gospel of Luke reflect such historical realities? Could the legend of the flight of Mary and Joseph to Egypt during Herod's persecution indicate that is where the family's support network came from? Could the original differences between Jews and Christians be comparable to the differences between Sunni and Shiite Muslims? Could Isaiah's prophecy of the birth of "the child" been not simply about Jesus, but about a new, putative dynastic family of wholly spiritual or sagelike kings who would survive the political holocaust of the coming centuries?

It is significant that the hardness of the way of kingship and of peoplehood which Isaiah lays out parabolically spills into wordplay over the meaning of "rocks" and "stumbling blocks." The "stone of stumbling," the "stone which the builders rejected," these and similar phrases are not only the heart of Christian self-understanding, they are metaphors related to the act of temple-building. As the Temple at Jerusalem is destroyed, the idea of a new spiritual or Sophianic temple emerges. It is the temple rejected by the Davidic rulers. It is the temple where the New Presence, the eschatological Shekinah, dwells. It is the temple that shall emerge when the physical temple of stones is torn down. It is, as Isaiah says, "a snare to those who live in Jerusalem."

42. See Joachim Theis, *Paulus als Weisheitslehrer: der Gekreuzigte und die Weisheit Gottes in 1 Kor 1–4* (Regensburg: Verlag Friedrich Pustet, 1991), 418.

4: The Divine Feminine

1. See Geoffrey Ashe, *The Virgin* (London: Routledge & Kegan Paul, 1976), 195.

2. For analyses of the Grail legend in the Middle Ages, see John Matthews, ed., *The Household of the Grail* (Northhamptonshire: Aquarian Press, 1990); Richard L. Harp, "The Christian Poetic of the Search for the Holy Grail," *Christian Scholar's Review* 4 (1975): 300–10; René Guénon, "The Sacred Heart and the Legend of the Holy Grail," *Studies in Comparative Religion* 16 (Summer-Autumn 1984): 234–41.

3. For an excellent discussion of this topic, see John C. Moore, *Love in Twelfth-Century France* (Philadelphia: University of Pennsylvania Press, 1972), 53–70. Other articles include David Carlson, "The Practical

Theology and the Date of the *De Laude Novae Militiae*," in John R. Sommerfeldt, ed., *Erudition at God's Service: Studies in Medieval Cistercian History*, XI (Kalamazoo, Mich.: Cistercian Publications, 1987), 133–47.

For an examination of the relationship between Bernardian theology and the Grail literature, see John H. Cleland, "Bernardian Ideas in Wolfram's *Parsival* about Christian War and Human Development," in E. Rozanne Elder and John R. Sommerfeldt, eds., *The Chimaera of His Age: Studies on Bernard of Clairvaux* (Kalamazoo, Mich.: Cistercian Publications, 1980), 39–61; Sister Isabel Mary, S.L.G., "The Knights of God: Citeaux and the Quest of the Holy Grail," in Sister Benedicta Ward, S.L.G., ed., *The Influence of Saint Bernard* (Oxford: SLG Press, 1976), 53–88.

4. The literature on the troubadours is extensive. Some of the more important works include Peter L. Allen, *The Art of Love: Amatory Fiction from Ovid to the Romance of the Rose* (Philadelphia: University of Pennsylvania Press, 1992); Joan M. Ferrante and George D. Economou, eds., *In Pursuit of Perfection: Courtly Love in Medieval Literature* (Port Washington, N.Y.: Kennikat Press, 1975); Jack Lindsay, *The Troubadours and Their World* (London: Frederick Mullter, 1976); John Frederick Rowbotham, *The Troubadours and Courts of Love* (London: Swan Sonnenschein & Co., 1895); Roger Boase, *The Origin and Meaning of Courtly Love* (Manchester: Manchester University Press, 1977); L. T. Topsfield, *Troubadours and Love* (Cambridge: Cambridge University Press, 1975); Francis Hueffer, *The Troubadours: Provençal Life and Literature in the Middle Ages* (London: Chatto & Windus, Piccadilly, 1978).

5. See Jonathan Sumption, *The Albigensian Crusade* (London: Faber & Faber, 1978); A. J. Forey, "The Military Orders and Holy War against Christians in the Thirteenth Century," *The English Historical Review* (January 1989): 1–24; J. Lee Shneidman and Conalee Levine-Shneidman, "The Albigensian Cathari" in David A. Halperin, ed., *Religion, Sect, and Cult* (London: John Wright, 1983), 45–58; John Hine Mundy, "Urban Society and Culture: Toulouse and Its Region," in Robert L. Benson and Giles Constable, eds., *Renaissance and Renewal in the Twelfth Century* (Oxford: Clarendon Press, 1982), 229–47.

6. *Lyrics of the Troubadours and Trouvères*, trans. Fredrick Goldin (Garden City, N.Y.: Anchor Books, 1973), 85.

7. Ibid., 367.

8. Ibid., 461.

9. *Andreas Capellanus on Love*, ed. and trans. P. G. Walsh (London: Gerald Duckworth & Co., 1982), 33.

10. Ibid., 121.

11. The notion of troubadour love as a neurotic and suicidal form of erotic romanticism has become a kind of conventional wisdom because of the work of Denis de Rougement. See his *Love in the Western World*, trans. Montgomery Belgion (New York: Harcourt, Brace & Co., 1940).

12. For an interesting article that traces Sophia theology throughout

some of the major thinkers of the Middle Ages, such as Bernard of Clair-vaux, Hildegard of Bingen, Henry Suso, and Julian of Norwich, see Barbara Newman, "Some Medieval Theologians and the Sophia Tradi-tion," *Downside Review* 108 (April 1990): 111–30.

13. A version of this argument can be found in Guénon, "The Sacred Heart," 238f. See also Francis Landy, "Beauty and the Enigma," *Journal for the Study of the Old Testament* 17 (1980): 55–106.

14. See Moore, *Love in Twelfth-Century France*, 51–70.

15. Marina Warner, *Alone of All Her Sex: The Myth and the Cult of the Virgin Mary* (New York: Alfred A. Knopf, 1976), 147.

16. Contemporary sociocultural studies of the cult of the Virgin in-clude the following: Michael P. Carroll, *The Cult of the Virgin Mary: Psy-chological Origins* (Princeton, N.J.: Princeton University Press, 1986); Andrew Greeley, *The Mary Myth: On the Femininity of God* (New York: Seabury Press, 1977); Ashe, *The Virgin*.

17. For studies of troubadour rhetoric and style, see Douglas Kelly, *Medieval Imagination: Rhetoric and the Poetry of Courtly Love* (Madison, Wis.: University of Wisconsin Press, 1978); Laura Kendrick, *The Game of Love: Troubadour Wordplay* (Berkeley, Calif.: University of California Press, 1988). For a study of related love literature, see P. G. Walsh, ed., *Love Lyrics from the Carmina Burana* (Chapel Hill, N.C.: University of North Carolina Press, 1993).

18. *Lyrics of the Troubadours*, 21.

19. *Lyrics of the Troubadours*, 83.

20. King Philip's motives in attacking the Templars are still the topic of much historical speculation. The lust for power and his coveting of the order's wealth are the usual reasons ascribed to his actions. However, there is also good evidence that Philip saw himself as a kind of final cru-sader, going to any extreme to purify the church and consolidating the rule of Christendom under a spiritual monarch. Philip's assault on the Templars, therefore, can be compared to the Albigensian Crusade a cen-tury earlier—the crusading ideal run amok and directed against Chris-tians themselves. For a consideration of this kind of thesis, see Elizabeth M. Hallam, "Philip the Fair and the Cult of Saint Louis," in Stuart Mews, ed., *Religion and National Identity: Papers Read at the Nineteenth Summer Meet-ing and the Twentieth Winter Meeting of the Ecclesiastical Historical Society* (Ox-ford: Basil Blackwell, 1982), 201–14.

21. For an overview of the Templar controversy, see Stephen Howarth, *The Knights Templar* (New York: Atheneum, 1982); Malcolm Barber, *The Trial of the Templars* (Cambridge: Cambridge University Press, 1978); Alan J. Forey, "The Beginning of Proceedings against Aragonese Templars," in Derek W. Lomax and David Mackenzie, eds., *God and Man in Medieval Spain* (Warminster: Aris & Phillips, 1989), 81–96; Indrikis Sterns, "Crime and Punishment among Teutonic Knights," *Speculum* 57 (1982):84–111; A. J. Forey, "The Military Orders in the Crusading Proposals of the Late-Thirteenth and Early-Fourteenth

Centuries," *Traditio,* vol. 36 (New York: Fordham University Press, 1980), 317–45; Karlhans Kluncker, "Die Templer: Geschichte und Geheimnis," *Zeitschrift für Religions- und Geistesgeschichte* 41 (1989): 215–47. The article by Kluncker should be treated cautiously, because it gives credence to many of the conspiratorial accusations of the church against the order.

22. See Baring and Cashford, *Myth of the Goddess,* 636, as well as Hugh Schonfield, *The Essene Odyssey* (Dorset: Element Books, 1984).

23. Baring and Cashford, *Myth of the Goddess,* 638.

24. Ibid.

25. This sort of argument is typical of the book by Baring and Cashford, esp. the section on Sophia (609–58). It also characterizes the earlier best-seller of Elaine Pagels, *The Gnostic Gospels* (New York: Random House, 1979).

26. For an excellent historical survey of the different versions of romantic Templarism, see Peter Partner, *The Murdered Magicians: The Templars and Their Myth* (Oxford: Oxford University Press, 1982).

5: Toward a Revelation of the Twin-Faced Godhead

1. *The New English Bible,* New Testament, 79.

2. Most scholars date Revelation during the reign of the Roman emperor Domitian, or around 80 C.E., which would have been right after the destruction of the Temple at Jerusalem.

3. "I, Jesus, have sent my angel to you with this testimony for the churches. I am the scion and offspring of David, the bright star of dawn" (Rev. 22:16).

4. See *The New English Bible,* New Testament, 331, fn. to 21:5.

5.   Cease to dwell on days gone by
   and to brood over past history.
   Here and now I will *do a new thing;*
      this moment it will break from the bud.
      Can you not perceive it?
I will make a way even through the wilderness
      and paths in the barren desert;
      the wild beasts shall do me honor,
      the wolf and the ostrich;
   for I will provide water in the wilderness
      and rivers in the barren desert,
      where my chosen people may drink.
   I have formed this people for myself
      and they shall proclaim my praises.
                              (Isa. 43:18–21, italics added)